Scrappy Bed Quilts

LEISURE ARTS®

CREATED FOR LEISURE ARTS BY HOUSE OF WHITE BIRCHES

Contents

SCRAPPY BED QUILTS ©2001, 2000, 1999, 1998, 1997 House of White Birches, 306 East Parr Road, Berne, IN 46711, (260) 589-4000. Customer_Service@whitebirches.com. Made in USA.

ISBN: 1-57486-357-6

CREDITS: Medallion Flower Quilt, page 38 provided by Classic Cottons.

Introduction

Longtime quilters are sure to have closets or bins filled to the brim with glorious scraps from dozens of projects or trips to fabric shops where the bargains were just too wonderful to ignore. It's reason enough for most of us to collect fabric just because we love the color or the print or the texture.

Dresden Plate

Lucy Loves Purple

Whether you choose to dig into your stash of scraps or make another trip to the shop to purchase brand-new fabrics, you'll love the splendid scrappy bed quilts in this book.

A scrappy quilt can have many looks. Some quilts use only fabrics in specific colors, such as Prairie Claw, which uses only red, black and gold scraps. Feeling blue? Then check out Am I Blue? on page 88 and Atlantis on page 93, both of which use only blue fabric.

Often our quilts remind us of special things and favorite places. The pastel print fabrics used in Taffy on page 105 will bring to mind the many colors of taffy candy. The lovely floral prints in Medallion Flower Quilt on page 38 bring back favorite memories of gardens and flowers.

Test your creative skills by putting together a quilt with dozens of fabric scraps. The quilt on page 100 uses 18 different fabrics, with three quilt blocks of each one. The Nine-Patch Scrap Quilt on page 76 has 180 different-colored blocks, guaranteed to empty your closet of those fabrics you've been saving for just the right place.

No matter which pattern you choose, you're sure to enjoy arranging, then re-arranging all those wonderful bits and pieces on your worktable before you begin to stitch. Quilting has never been this much fun!

Nighttime Scrappy Stars

Tree Of Life

BY JILL REBER

Make the leaves on these trees in seasonal colors, changing them for every block, and you'll have a quilt for all seasons. While making the trees may look like a daunting task because of the number of leaves in each tree block, take it one block at a time. Before you know it, you'll have finished a most beautiful quilt.

Tree of Life

5" x 78 7/8"

5" x 90 7/8"

Tree of Life
Placement Diagram
Approximately 79" x 101"

Tree of Life

Tree of Life
13 1/2" x 13 1/2" Block

Project Specifications
Quilt Size: Approximately 79" x 101"
Block Size: 13½" x 13½"
Number of Blocks: 18

Fabric & Batting
- 1 yard brown print for tree trunks
- 1¼ yards tan print for sashing strips
- 4 fat eighths each burgundy, green, gold, brown, tan and rust prints
- 1¼ yards green solid for sashing squares and borders
- 3 yards muslin
- 3 yards green print for borders and fill-in triangles
- Backing 83" x 105"
- Batting 83" x 105"
- 10½ yards self-made or purchased binding

Supplies & Tools
- Neutral color all-purpose thread
- Basic sewing tools and supplies, rotary cutter, ruler and cutting mat

Instructions
1. Prepare template for A using pattern piece given. Cut as directed on template; set aside.

2. Cut three strips muslin 6⅞" by fabric width; sub-cut into 6⅞"-square segments. Cut each segment in half on one diagonal to make B triangles. You will need 36 B triangles.

3. Cut 17 strips muslin 2⅜" by fabric width; subcut into 2⅜"-square segments. Cut each segment in half on one diagonal to make C triangles. You will need 576 C triangles.

4. Cut one strip muslin 3⅞" by fabric width; subcut into 3⅞"-square segments. Cut each segment in half on one diagonal to make D triangles. You will need 18 D triangles.

5. Cut four strips muslin 2" by fabric width; subcut into 2"-square segments for E. You will need 72 E squares.

6. Cut two strips brown print 5⅜" by fabric width; subcut into 5⅜"-square segments. Cut each square on one diagonal to make F triangles; you will need 18 F triangles.

Tree of Life

7. Cut two strips brown print 5¾" by fabric width; sub-cut into 2½" segments for G. You will need 18 G pieces.

8. Cut one strip brown print 2" by fabric width; sub-cut into 2"-square segments. Cut each segment in half on one diagonal to make H triangles; you will need 36 H triangles.

9. To make colored triangles for C, cut 360 squares fall prints 2⅜" x 2⅜", cutting 60 from each same-color family—green, brown, gold, etc.—for three Tree of Life blocks of each color. Cut each square in half on one diagonal to make 720 C triangles.

10. Sew a colored C triangle to a muslin C triangle; repeat for all C triangles.

11. To piece one block, select 40 C triangle/squares from one color family. Arrange in rows with B triangles and E squares as shown in Figure 1 to make units. Join pieces in rows; join rows to make units for treetop section.

12. To make tree base, sew H to A and AR; join the two pieced units with G. Sew D and F to ends as shown in Figure 2.

13. Join the units pieced in steps 11 and 12 to complete one block as shown in Figure 3.

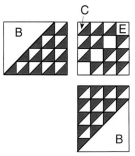

Figure 1
Arrange C units, B triangles and E squares in rows as shown.

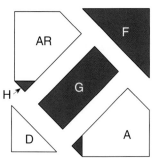

Figure 2
Join pieces to make tree base as shown.

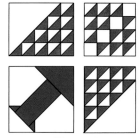

Figure 3
Join pieced units to complete 1 block.

14. Cut three strips tan print 14" by fabric width; subcut into 2½" segments for sashing strips. You will need 48 sashing strips.

15. Cut two strips green solid 2½" by fabric width; subcut into 2½"-square segments for sashing squares. You will need 31 squares.

16. Cut three squares green print 20¼" x 20¼"; cut each square in half on both diagonals to make side fill-in triangles. You will need 10 of these triangles.

17. Cut one strip green solid 26" by fabric width; subcut into 2" segments for triangle borders. You will need 10 strips.

18. Center and sew a 2" x 26" strip green solid to the bottom of each side fill-in triangle; trim excess as shown in Figure 4.

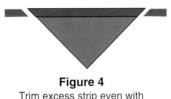

Figure 4
Trim excess strip even with
edges of side fill-in triangle.

19. Cut two squares 10¼" x 10¼" green print; cut each square on one diagonal to make corner triangles. You will need four of these triangles.

20. Cut eight strips green solid 2" x 15". Sew a strip to both short edges of each corner triangle; trim excess even with triangle referring to Figure 5.

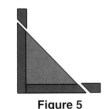

Figure 5
Trim excess strips even with
edges of corner triangles.

21. Join five blocks with six 2½" x 14" sashing strips beginning and ending with a strip; repeat for two

strips. Join three blocks with four 2½" x 14" sashing strips beginning and ending with a strip; repeat for two strips. Sew a 2½" x 14" sashing strip to opposite sides of one block as shown in Figure 6; repeat. Press all seams toward strips.

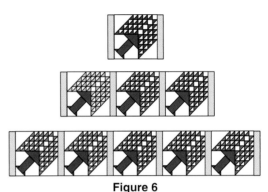

Figure 6
Join blocks with sashing
strips as shown.

22. Join six 2½" x 14" sashing strips with seven 2½" x 2½" sashing squares. Repeat with five strips and six squares twice and three strips and four squares twice. Sew a square to each end of the two remaining strips. Press all seams toward sashing strips.

23. Arrange block rows and sashing strip rows with side fill-in and corner triangles as shown in Figure 7. Join rows to complete pieced center. Press seams in one direction.

24. Cut and piece two strips green print 5½" x 79⅜" and two strips 5½" x 91⅜". Sew the longer strips to

Tree of Life

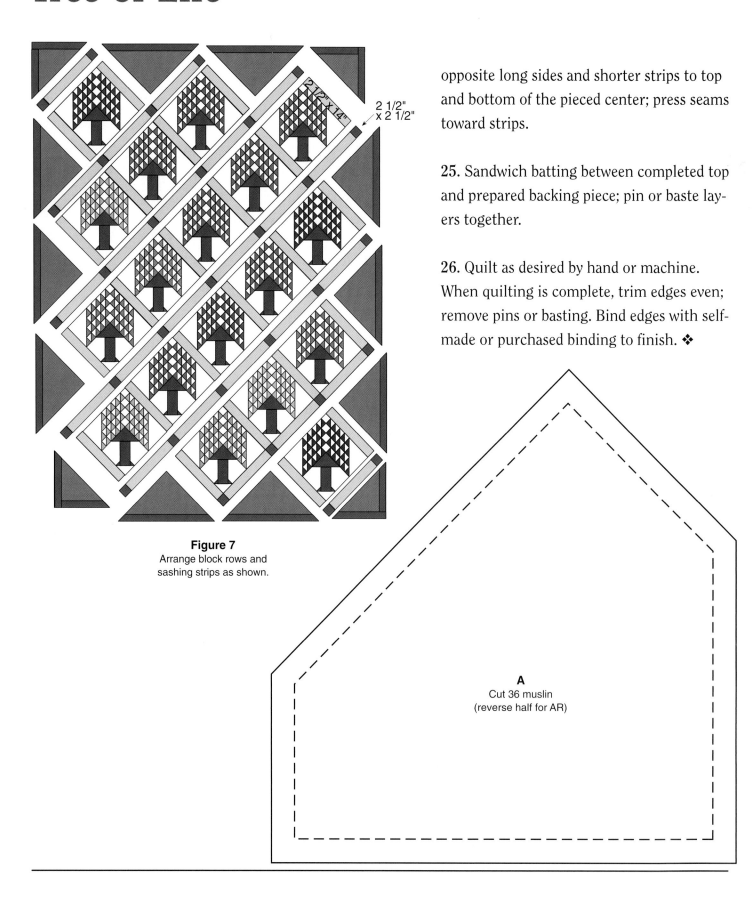

2 1/2" x 14"

2 1/2" x 2 1/2"

Figure 7
Arrange block rows and
sashing strips as shown.

A
Cut 36 muslin
(reverse half for AR)

opposite long sides and shorter strips to top
and bottom of the pieced center; press seams
toward strips.

25. Sandwich batting between completed top
and prepared backing piece; pin or baste layers together.

26. Quilt as desired by hand or machine.
When quilting is complete, trim edges even;
remove pins or basting. Bind edges with self-
made or purchased binding to finish. ❖

Double Four-Patch

BY LUCY A. FAZELY

The designer used reproduction shirting prints for the background of this quilt and then added other scraps to complete the pattern. This is the perfect home for all of those scraps saved from other projects. If you use the quick method given here, you'll be able to make this bed quilt in a weekend. If quick methods aren't your preference, take your time using the traditional template method. Either way, the results will be beautiful.

Double Four-Patch

Project Specifications
Quilt Size: 46" x 58"
Block Size: 6" x 6"
Number of Blocks: 48

Fabric & Batting
- ⅛ yard each of 5 prints: brown, black or green
- ⅛ yard each of 3 burgundy prints and 3 blue prints
- ⅙ yard each of 10 shirting prints for background
- ⅜ yard mauve print
- ⅝ yard dark burgundy print
- Backing 49" x 61"
- Batting 49" x 61"
- 6 yards self-made or purchased binding

Supplies & Tools
- Neutral color all-purpose thread

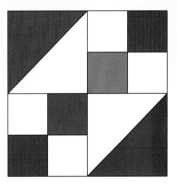

Double Four-Patch
6" x 6" Block

- Basic sewing supplies and tools, rotary cutter, ruler and cutting mat

Quick Method
1. Cut one strip each from burgundy and blue prints 3⅞" by fabric width; subcut each strip into 3⅞" segments. Cut each segment on one diagonal to make A triangles. You will need 48 each burgundy and blue print A triangles.

2. Cut one strip each of 10 shirting prints 3⅞" by fabric width; subcut into 3⅞" segments. Cut each segment on one diagonal to make A triangles. You will need 96 A triangles.

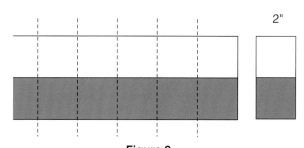

Figure 2
Subcut each strip into 2" segments.

3. Sew a shirting print A to a burgundy or blue print A as shown in Figure 1; repeat for 96 A units.

4. Cut a total of 10 strips 2" by fabric width from brown, black or green prints and one strip from each shirting print.

Figure 1
Sew a shirting background print A to a burgundy or blue print A to make A units.

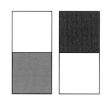

Figure 3
Join 2 segments as shown to make Four-Patch units.

5. Sew a brown, black or green print strip to a shirting print strip with right sides together along length; repeat to make 10 strip sets. Press seams toward darker fabrics.

6. Subcut each strip set into 2" segments as shown in Figure 2; repeat for 192 segments.

7. Join two segments as shown in Figure 3 to make Four-Patch units; press seams in one direction. Repeat for 96 Four-Patch units.

8. Join two Four-Patch units with one burgundy A unit and one blue A unit to make a Double Four-Patch block as shown in Figure 4; repeat for 48 blocks.

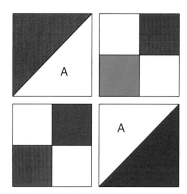

Figure 4
Join 2 Four-Patch units with 2 A units to make a Double Four-Patch block.

9. Join six blocks to make an A row as shown in Figure 5; repeat for four A rows. Press seams in one direction.

10. Join six blocks to make a B row as shown in Figure 6; repeat for four B rows. Press seams in one direction.

Double Four-Patch

3" x 40"

2" x 36"

3" x 58"

2" x 52"

2" x 36"

Double Four-Patch
Placement Diagram
46" x 58"

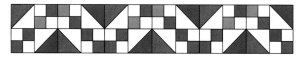

Figure 5
Join 6 blocks to make an A row.

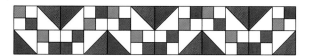

Figure 6
Join 6 blocks to make a B row.

11. Join A and B rows, beginning with an A row and referring to the Placement Diagram; press seams in one direction.

12. Cut and piece two strips each mauve print 2½" x 36½" and 2½" x 52½". Sew the shorter strips to the top and bottom and longer strips to opposite long sides; press seams toward strips.

13. Cut and piece two strips each dark burgundy print 3½" x 40½" and 3½" x 58½". Sew the shorter strips to the top and bottom and longer strips to opposite long sides; press seams toward strips.

14. Sandwich batting between completed top and prepared backing piece; pin or baste layers together to hold flat for quilting.

15. Quilt as desired by hand or machine. When quilting is complete, trim edges even; remove pins or basting.

16. Bind edges with self-made or purchased binding to finish.

Traditional Method

1. Prepare templates using pattern pieces given. Cut as directed on each piece.

2. Sew a dark print B to a light print B; repeat for 192 B units.

3. Complete blocks and quilt referring to steps 3 and 7–16 for Quick Method. ❖

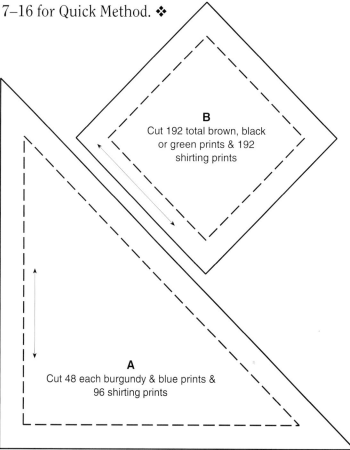

B
Cut 192 total brown, black or green prints & 192 shirting prints

A
Cut 48 each burgundy & blue prints & 96 shirting prints

Dresden Plate

BY LUCY A. FAZELY

This was a favorite pattern of the 1930s, and it is reproduced here using reproduction prints from that era. If you don't have a stash of reproduction fabrics, any prints can be used to make this beautiful quilt. Because you need over 24 different fabrics to create the plates, this could be a great home for your stash of fabrics.

Dresden Plate

Dresden Plate
Placement Diagram
44" x 62"

Dresden Plate

Project Specifications

Quilt Size: 44" x 62"

Block Size: 16" x 16"

Number of Blocks: 6

Fabric & Batting

- ⅛ yard each 24 different 1930s reproduction fabrics
- 1¾ yards each lavender solid and green reproduction floral print
- 2 yards unbleached muslin
- Needled cotton batting 48" x 66"
- Backing 48" x 66"
- 6¼ yards self-made or purchased binding

Supplies & Tools

- All-purpose thread to match fabrics
- Template plastic or purchased templates
- Basic sewing supplies and tools

Instructions

1. Prepare templates using pattern pieces given or use purchased templates. Cut as directed on each piece for one block.

2. To piece one Dresden Plate block, join two A pieces sewing to dots marked on A as shown in Figure

Dresden Plate
16" x 16" Block

1; repeat for eight A-A units. Join two A-A units to make quarter sections. Join two quarter sections to make half of block; repeat. Join two half-sections to complete Dresden circle.

Figure 1
Join A pieces as shown.

3. Turn under top edges of each A piece along seam allowance from dot to dot, carefully keeping curved shape of A.

4. Cut six squares muslin 16½" x 16½". Fold each square in half from top to bottom and side to side; press to form crease lines to mark centers.

5. Arrange one pieced A unit on one muslin square, lining up the center line on A with side

and top and bottom creases as shown in Figure 2. Pin or baste in place.

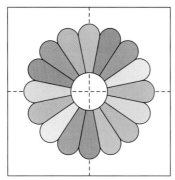

Figure 2
Arrange stitched A unit on background block, matching centers as shown.

2 1/2" x 16 1/2"

Figure 3
Join blocks with sashing strips to make a row as shown.

6. Appliqué A units in place by hand or machine. Baste inside raw edges to muslin square; repeat for six blocks.

7. Turn under edge of B circles, making a smooth curve; hand-appliqué in place over the center of the appliquéd A units.

8. Cut six strips lavender solid 2½" x 16½". Join three blocks with two strips to make a row as shown in Figure 3; repeat for a second row.

9. Cut three strips lavender solid 2½" x 52½". Referring to Placement Diagram, join the block rows with these strips, beginning and ending with a strip; press seams toward strips.

10. Cut two strips lavender solid 2½" x 38½". Sew a strip to the top and bottom of the pieced center; press seams toward strips.

11. Cut two strips green reproduction floral print 3½" x 56½". Sew a strip to opposite long sides of pieced center; press seams toward strips. Cut two more strips green reproduction floral print 3½" x 44½"; sew a strip to the top and bottom of pieced center. Press seams toward strips.

12. Sandwich batting between completed top and prepared backing piece. Pin or baste layers together to hold flat.

13. Quilt as desired by hand or machine. When quilting is complete, trim edges even. Bind with self-made or purchased binding to finish. ❖

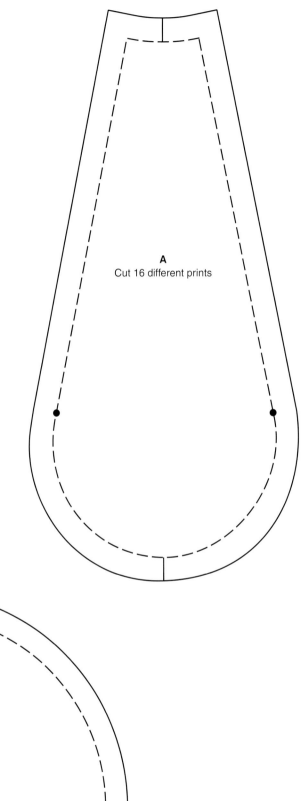

A
Cut 16 different prints

B
Cut 1 lavender solid

Place line on fold

Traveling Leaves

BY BONNIE GHEESLING

The designer of this quilt so wanted to capture memories of a trip to New England that she gathered leaves along the way. When she arrived home, the leaves were used as patterns to create a memory quilt of her travels. You can copy her memories or you may prefer to use your leaf patterns to create your own memory quilt. The leaves in this quilt are machine appliquéd. This quilt is the perfect way to enjoy a trip forever.

Traveling Leaves

Traveling Leaves
Placement Diagram
78" x 90"

Traveling Leaves

Project Specifications

Quilt Size: 78" x 90"

Fabric & Batting

- Variety of scraps to match leaf colors
- Muslin 48½" x 60½" for center background
- ¾ yard peach solid
- 1⅝ yards leaf print
- 1¾ yards green solid
- Backing 82" x 94"
- Batting 82" x 94"
- 9¾ yards self-made or purchased binding
- 3 yards fusible web
- 2½ yards fabric stabilizer

Supplies & Tools

- All-purpose thread to match fabrics
- Basic sewing tools and supplies

Instructions

1. Use your own leaves or the shapes given to create leaf templates.

2. Trace the leaf shapes onto the paper side of the fusible web. Cut out shapes, leaving a margin around each one. *Note: The number of leaves used will vary with every quilt. The quilt shown uses over 90 leaves.*

3. Fuse the paper shapes to the wrong side of the leaf-colored scraps; cut out on traced lines. Remove paper backing.

4. Fold the 48½" x 60½" muslin background and crease to mark centers.

5. Arrange the leaf shapes on the background at random, holding a few leaves aside to overlap onto border strips.

6. When satisfied with arrangement, fuse leaves in place.

7. Pin fabric stabilizer behind leaf shapes. Using all-purpose thread, machine-appliqué leaves in place. When all leaves are stitched in place, remove fabric stabilizer.

8. Cut and piece two strips each 3½" x 48½" and 3½" x 66½" peach solid; sew the shorter strips to the top and bottom and longer strips to opposite sides of the appliquéd center. Press seams toward strips.

9. Cut and piece two strips each 6½" x 54½" and 6½" x 78½" leaf print; sew the shorter strips to the top and bottom and longer strips to opposite sides of the appliquéd center. Press seams toward strips.

10. Cut and piece two strips each 6½" x 66½" and

Traveling Leaves

6½" x 90½" green solid; sew the shorter strips to the top and bottom and longer strips to opposite sides of the appliquéd center. Press seams toward strips.

11. Fuse remaining leaves to border strips at random referring to the Placement Diagram and photo of quilt for positioning suggestions. Appliqué in place as in step 7.

12. Sandwich batting between completed top and prepared backing piece; pin or baste to hold layers together.

13. Quilt leaf vines as marked on patterns and the remainder of the background and borders as desired by hand or machine.

14. When quilting is complete, trim edges even and remove pins or basting. Bind edges with self-made or purchased binding to finish. ❖

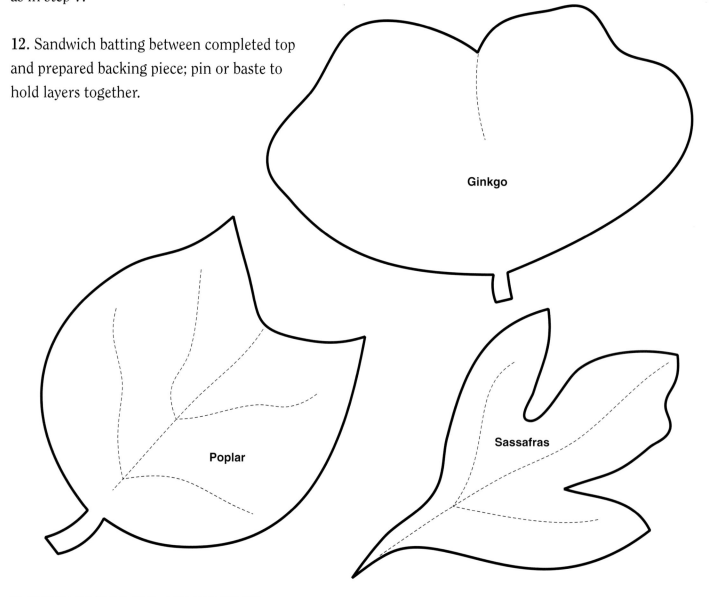

Ginkgo

Poplar

Sassafras

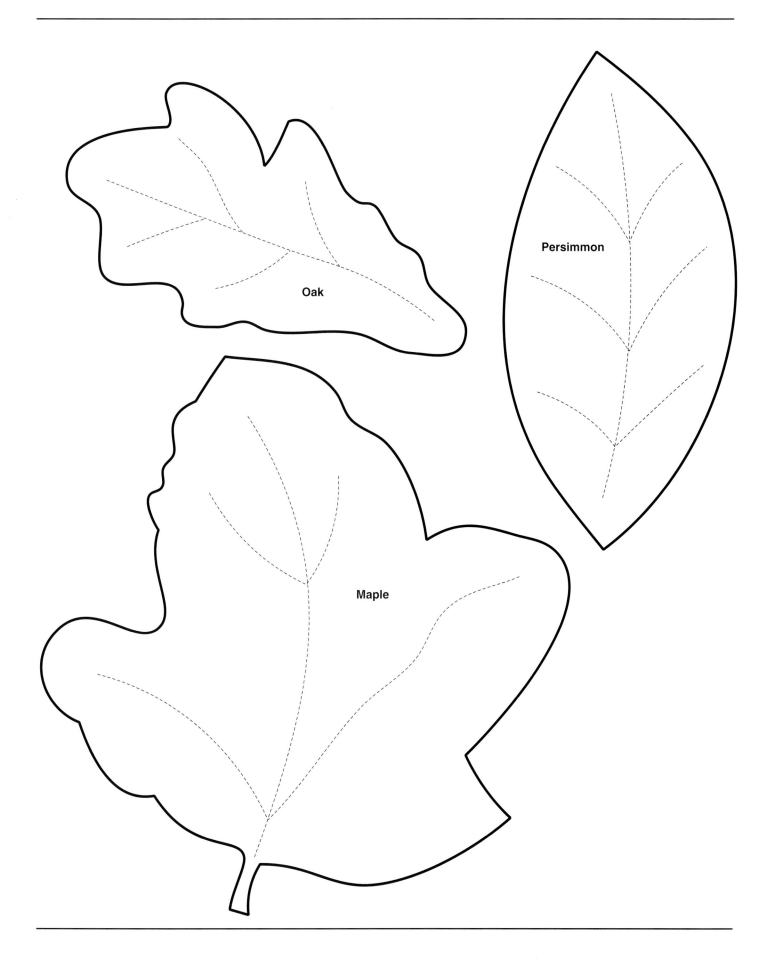

Oak

Persimmon

Maple

Traveling Leaves

Oak

Holly

Oak

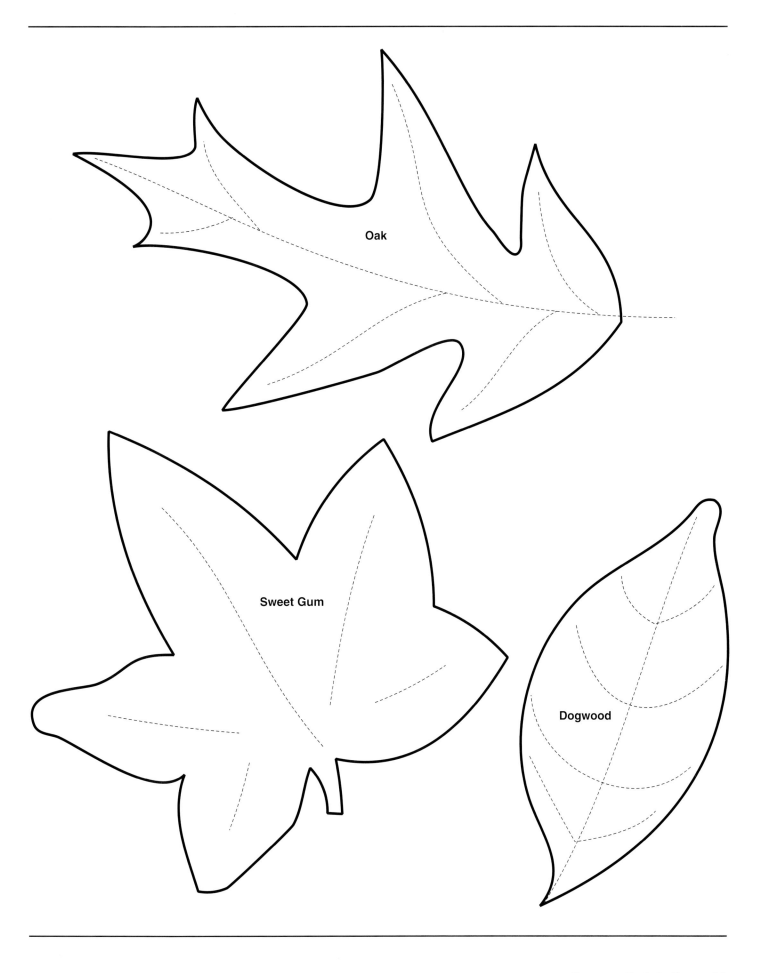

Oak

Sweet Gum

Dogwood

Nighttime Scrappy Stars

BY LINDA DENNER

This quilt's designer challenged herself to put together the scraps she had collected in over 25 years of quiltmaking into a pleasing quilt. She began by refining her scrap piles into 2⅞" squares and 2½" squares of assorted colors. She then created 20 brightly colored stars with lights in the background and set them on point. Alternate stars were reversed with stars made of off-white and white prints placed on a background fabric of dark navy prints. The finished quilt is a fantastic example of how a scrap quilt can be created.

Nighttime Scrappy Stars

6" x 68 7/8"

6" x 68 1/4"

Nighttime Scrappy Stars
Placement Diagram
68 7/8" x 80 1/4"

Nighttime Scrappy Stars

Four-Patch Star
8" x 8" Block

Project Specifications

Quilt Size: 68⅞" x 80¼"

Block Size: 8" x 8"

Number of Blocks: 32

Fabric & Batting

- 1 yard assorted navy scraps
- 2 yards navy print
- 2¼ yards assorted dark-value scraps
- 2¾ yards assorted white-on-white and cream-on-cream light scraps
- Backing 73" x 84"
- Batting 73" x 84"
- 8¾ yards self-made or purchased binding

Supplies & Tools

- Neutral color all-purpose thread
- White quilting thread
- Basic sewing tools and supplies, newspaper, rotary cutter, ruler and cutting mat

Instructions

1. Cut 80 squares each dark and light scraps 2⅞" x 2⅞". Cut each square in half on one diagonal to make triangle/squares.

2. Sew a light triangle to a dark triangle to make a triangle/square as shown in Figure 1; repeat for 160 triangle/squares.

Figure 1
Sew a light triangle to a dark triangle to make a triangle/square.

3. Cut 80 squares each dark and light scraps 2½" x 2½" for A.

4. Join two triangle/squares with two light A squares to make a pieced unit as shown in Figure 2; repeat for 40 units.

Figure 2
Join 2 triangle/squares with 2 light A squares to make a pieced unit.

Nighttime Scrappy Stars

5. Join two triangle/squares with two dark A squares to make a pieced unit as shown in Figure 3; repeat for 40 units.

Figure 3
Join 2 triangle/squares with 2 dark A squares to make a pieced unit.

6. Join four units to make a dark/light Four-Patch Star block as shown in Figure 4; repeat for 20 blocks.

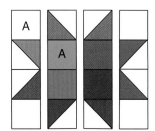

Figure 4
Join 4 units to make a Four-Patch Star block.

7. Cut 48 squares each 2⅞" x 2⅞" and 2½" x 2½" navy and light scraps. Cut each 2⅞" square in half on one diagonal to make triangle/squares.

8. Join pieces to make a light/dark version of the Four-Patch Star block as shown in Figure 5; repeat for 12 blocks.

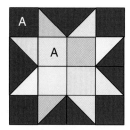

Figure 5
Join pieces to make a light/dark version of the Four-Patch Star block.

9. Cut four squares navy print 12⅝" x 12⅝"; cut each square on both diagonals as shown in Figure 6 to make side triangles. You will need 14 side triangles.

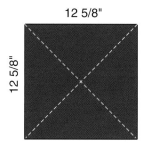

Figure 6
Cut 4 squares navy print 12 5/8" x 12 5/8"; cut each square on both diagonals.

10. Cut two squares navy print 6⅝" x 6⅝". Cut each square on one diagonal to make corner triangles.

11. Arrange blocks in diagonal rows with side and corner triangles as shown in Figure 7; join in rows. Add corner triangles to finish the pieced center; press seams in one direction.

12. Cut nine squares newspaper 12⅝" x 12⅝". Cut each square in half through both diagonals to make triangles. Discard extras to make 34 triangles.

Figure 7
Arrange blocks in diagonal rows
with side and corner triangles.

13. Mark the long side of a paper triangle with ¼"
seam allowance. Fold the paper triangle in half
along the long side to find the center; crease. Mark
a 2" triangle centered on this spot using a pencil as
shown in Figure 8.

14. Using the ruler, mark a 1" line parallel to one
side and ending on that side of one leg of the triangle. Repeat this on the remaining side to repre-
sent the two logs of the Log Cabin. Mark a third 1"
strip next to the first and a fourth log adjacent to the
second. Continue marking the paper in this manner
until the paper is covered. You will have three logs
on each side of the triangle as shown in Figure 9.

15. Cut the fabric strips for the Log Cabin triangular
border 1½" in width from a variety of light and dark
scraps. Cut nine squares each dark and light scraps
2⅞" x 2⅞". Cut each square on one diagonal to
make center triangles.

16. Pin a fabric triangle on the unmarked side of the
paper triangle in the marked triangle space. Pin a
fabric strip right sides together with one side of the
triangle as shown in Figure 10; stitch along marked
line on the marked side of the paper triangle using a
short stitch length.

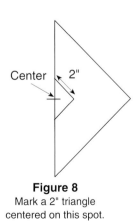

Center ↗ 2"

Figure 8
Mark a 2" triangle
centered on this spot.

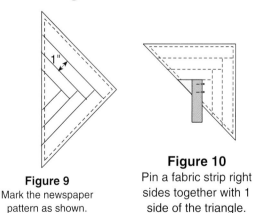

1"

Figure 9
Mark the newspaper
pattern as shown.

Figure 10
Pin a fabric strip right
sides together with 1
side of the triangle.

Nighttime Scrappy Stars

17. When stitching is complete, turn paper over; trim excess strip even with triangle and press strip flat. Continue adding and trimming strips using light strips on light blocks and dark strips on dark blocks until paper triangle is covered; trim excess even with edge of paper. Repeat for 18 light and 18 dark half Log Cabin triangles.

18. Cut three strips each light and dark prints 1½" x 25" and one strip each 2" x 25". Join the three light strips with right sides together along length with the 2" light strip to make a strip set; press seams in one direction. Repeat with dark strips.

19. Prepare template using pattern given. Cut strip sets into triangles, aligning template lines with strip seams as shown in Figure 11; repeat for four light and four dark triangles.

Figure 11
Cut strip sets into triangles aligning lines with strip seams.

20. Join four dark and three light half Log Cabin triangles to make a strip as shown in Figure 12; repeat for two strips. Press seams toward dark triangles. Sew a light triangle to each end of each strip, again referring to Figure 12.

Figure 12
Join 4 dark and 3 light half Log Cabin triangles to make a strip; add a light triangle to each end.

21. Sew a strip to the top and bottom of the pieced center referring to the Placement Diagram for positioning of strips.

22. Join five dark and six light half Log Cabin triangles to make a strip as shown in Figure 13; repeat for two strips. Press seams toward dark triangles. Sew a dark triangle to each strip, again referring to Figure 13.

Figure 13
Join 5 dark and 6 light half Log Cabin triangles to make a strip; add a dark triangle to each end.

23. Sew a strip to the remaining sides of the pieced center; press seams toward strips.

24. Cut two strips each navy print 6½" x 68¾ and 6½" x 69⅜". Sew the shorter strips to the longer sides and the longer strips to the top and bottom; press seams toward strips.

25. Sandwich batting between completed top and prepared backing piece; pin or baste layers together.

26. Quilt as desired by hand or machine. *Note: The sample shown was professionally machine-quilted with white quilting thread in an all-over meandering design.*

27. When quilting is complete, trim edges even. Remove pins or basting. Bind edges with self-made or purchased binding to finish. ❖

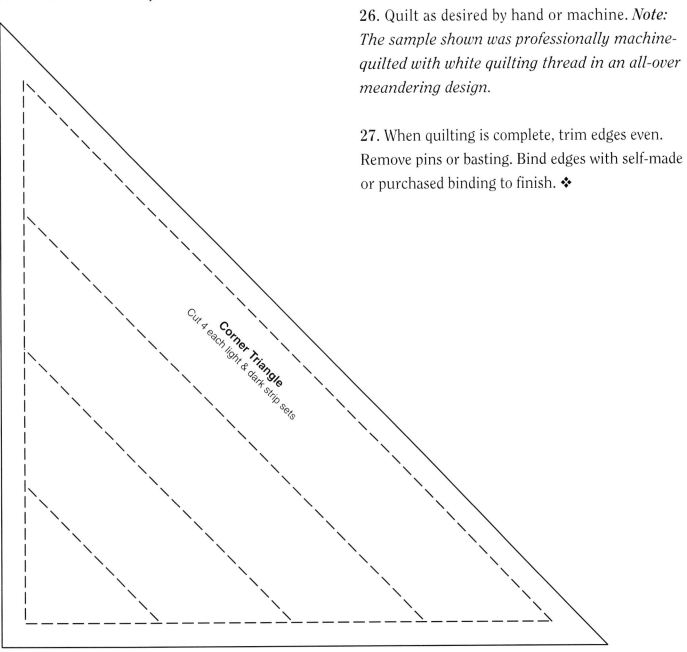

Corner Triangle
Cut 4 each light & dark strip sets

Medallion Flower Quilt

BY MICHELE CRAWFORD

If you take all the floral fabrics in your collection and follow the step-by-step instructions, you can re-create this stunning flower quilt without actually making a flower. Because the quilt uses different blocks, it is a wonderful project for anyone who tends to get bored making the same block again and again.

Medallion Flower Quilt

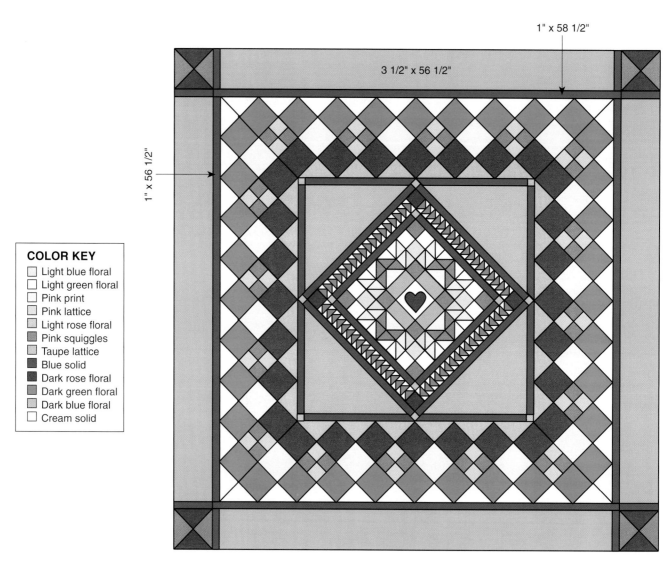

1" x 58 1/2"

3 1/2" x 56 1/2"

1" x 56 1/2"

COLOR KEY
- ☐ Light blue floral
- ☐ Light green floral
- ☐ Pink print
- ☐ Pink lattice
- ☐ Light rose floral
- ☐ Pink squiggles
- ☐ Taupe lattice
- ☐ Blue solid
- ☐ Dark rose floral
- ☐ Dark green floral
- ☐ Dark blue floral
- ☐ Cream solid

Medallion Flower Quilt
Placement Diagram
65 1/2" x 65 1/2"

Medallion Flower Quilt

Friendship Star
16" x 16" Block

Project Specifications

Quilt Size: 65½" x 65½"
Block Size: 16" x 16"
Number of Blocks: 1

Fabric & Batting

- ⅛ yard light blue floral
- ⅛ yard pink print
- ⅙ yard pink lattice
- ⅓ yard light green floral
- ⅓ yard light rose floral
- ⅜ yard pink squiggles
- ½ yard taupe lattice
- ⅝ yard dark rose floral
- ⅞ yard blue solid
- 1 yard dark green floral
- 1 yard cream solid
- 1⅜ yards dark blue floral
- Backing 70" x 70"
- Batting 70" x 70"
- 1 batting square 4" x 4"

Supplies & Tools

- Blue, pink and natural all-purpose thread
- Off-white quilting thread
- Basic sewing tools and supplies, rotary cutter, ruler and cutting mat

Instructions

Note: Use a ¼" seam allowance unless otherwise indicated. Sew pieces with right sides together and raw edges even using matching thread. Press seam allowances toward the darkest fabric unless otherwise indicated.

1. Prepare templates using pattern pieces given; cut as directed on each piece.

2. To piece the Friendship Star center block, sew B to two sides of the cream solid A. Sew a pink squiggles C to each end of two B pieces; sew the C-B units to remaining sides of A referring to Figure 1.

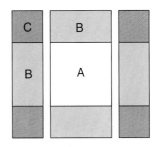

Figure 1
Sew the C-B units to remaining sides of A.

3. Sew a pink squiggles E to both short sides of D; repeat for four E-D units.

Medallion Flower Quilt

4. Sew a light blue floral E to a pink print E; repeat for eight blue/pink E-E units.

5. Sew a pink print E to a cream solid E; repeat for eight cream/pink E-E units.

6. Sew a pink squiggles E to a cream solid E; repeat for eight squiggles/cream E-E units.

7. Sew a blue/pink E-E unit to each end of an E-D unit. Join two cream/pink E-E units with two squiggles/cream E-E units as shown in Figure 2; sew to the E-D unit as shown in Figure 3. Repeat for four units.

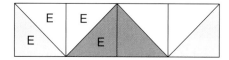

Figure 2
Join 2 cream/pink E-E units with 2 squiggles/cream E-E units as shown.

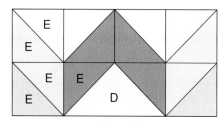

Figure 3
Sew the pieced E-E units to the E-D unit as shown.

8. Sew an E-D unit to opposite sides of the A-B-C unit as shown in Figure 4.

9. Join two cream solid C squares with a pink squiggles and a light blue floral C square to make a Four-Patch unit as shown in Figure 5. Sew a Four-Patch unit to each end of each remaining E-D unit as shown in Figure 6. Sew these units to the A-B-C-D-E unit to complete the Friendship Star center block.

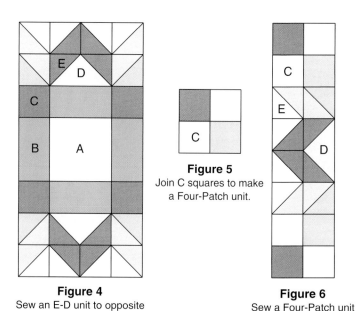

Figure 4
Sew an E-D unit to opposite sides of the A-B-C unit.

Figure 5
Join C squares to make a Four-Patch unit.

Figure 6
Sew a Four-Patch unit to each end of each remaining E-D unit.

10. Cut four strips blue solid 1½" x 16½". Sew a blue solid strip to opposite sides of the pieced center block; press. Sew an F square to each end of the two remaining strips and sew to remaining sides of the pieced center block; press.

11. Sew an H triangle to each short side of G to make a Flying Geese unit as shown in Figure 7; repeat for 72 units.

Figure 7
Sew an H triangle to each short side of G to make a Flying Geese unit.

12. Join 18 Flying Geese units as shown in Figure 8 to make a strip; repeat for four strips. Sew a strip to opposite sides of the pieced center. Sew a dark rose floral C square to each end of the remaining two strips and sew a strip to remaining sides of the pieced center; press.

Figure 8
Join 18 Flying Geese units as shown to make a strip.

13. Cut four strips blue solid 1½" x 22½". Sew a blue solid strip to opposite sides of the pieced center block; press. Sew an F square to each end of the two remaining strips and sew to remaining sides of the pieced center block; press.

14. Cut two squares taupe lattice 16½" x 16½". Cut each square in half on one diagonal to make four I triangles.

15. Cut eight strips blue solid 1½" x 18". Sew a blue solid strip to one short side of an I triangle, leaving excess on one end as shown in Figure 9; trim excess following the angle of I, again referring to Figure 9.

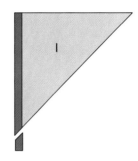

Figure 9
Sew a blue solid strip to 1 short side of an I triangle, leaving excess on 1 end as shown; trim excess following the angle of I.

16. Sew an F square to one end of one strip. Sew this strip to the remaining short side of I and trim as in step 15 referring to Figure 10; repeat for each of the I triangles.

17. Sew a bordered I triangle to each side of the pieced center as shown in Figure 11; press.

Medallion Flower Quilt

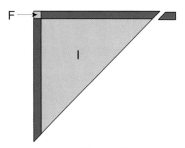

Figure 10
Sew the pieced strip to the
remaining short side of I and trim.

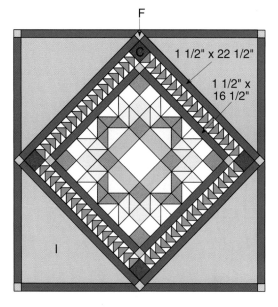

1 1/2" x 22 1/2"

1 1/2" x
16 1/2"

Figure 11
Sew a bordered I triangle to
each side of the pieced center.

19. Join one each dark rose floral, light green floral and dark green floral A squares with light pink floral and cream solid K triangles to make a B unit as shown in Figure 13; repeat for 12 B units.

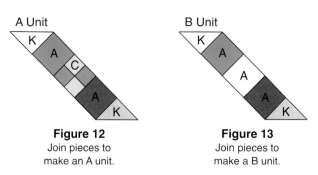

Figure 12
Join pieces to
make an A unit.

Figure 13
Join pieces to
make a B unit.

20. Join three A units with three B units as shown in Figure 14; repeat for four A-B units.

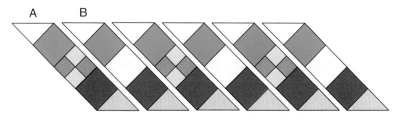

Figure 14
Join 3 A units with 3 B units as shown.

18. Join two pink squiggles C squares with two pink lattice C squares to make a Four-Patch unit. Join with one each dark rose floral and dark green floral A squares and light rose floral and cream solid K triangles to make an A unit as shown in Figure 12; repeat for 12 A units.

21. Join the remaining A and J pieces and Four-Patch units as shown in Figure 15 to make a C unit; repeat for four C units. Sew a C unit to one end of each A-B unit as shown in Figure 16.

22. Sew an A-B-C unit to each side of the pieced center, mitering seams at corners as shown in Figure 17.

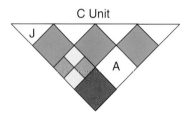

C Unit

Figure 15
Join the remaining A
and J pieces and Four-
Patch units as shown
to make a C unit.

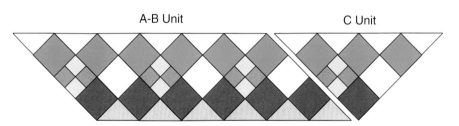

A-B Unit   C Unit

Figure 16
Sew a C unit to 1 end of each A-B unit.

23. Cut and piece two strips each blue solid 1½" x 57" and 1½" x 59". Sew the shorter strips to opposite sides of the pieced center and the longer strips to the remaining sides; press seams toward strips.

24. Cut and piece four strips dark blue floral 4" x 57".

25. Sew K to each end of each strip; sew one of these K strips to two opposite sides of the pieced center.

26. Join two pink squiggles and two dark rose floral L triangles as shown in Figure 18; repeat for four L triangle units.

Figure 17
Sew an A-B-C unit to each side of the
pieced center, mitering seams at corners.

L

Figure 18
Join 2 pink
squiggles and 2
dark rose floral
L triangles.

27. Sew an L triangle unit to opposite ends of the remaining K strips as shown in Figure 19. Sew

Medallion Flower Quilt

one of these strips to each remaining side of the pieced center to complete the pieced top; press.

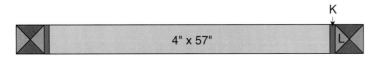

Figure 19
Sew an L triangle unit to opposite ends of a K strip.

28. Sandwich batting between completed top and prepared backing piece; pin or baste layers together to hold flat.

29. Quilt as desired by hand or machine using off-white quilting thread.

30. When quilting is complete, trim edges even and remove pins or basting.

31. Cut seven strips dark blue floral 1½" by fabric width. Sew strips together on short ends to make one long strip for binding. Press under ½" on one long edge. Sew binding strip to outside edges of quilt, mitering corners and overlapping ends. Turn to backside; hand-stitch in place.

32. Cut one 4" x 4" square each dark rose floral and cream solid. Center the wrong side of the dark

rose floral on the 4" x 4" batting square. Center the cream solid square right sides together with the dark rose floral square. Center the heart pattern given on the cream solid square; pin.

33. Topstitch around the outside of the heart pattern. Remove the heart pattern. Cut a ⅛" seam allowance around the outside of the stitched line; clip curves.

34. Cut a small slit in the center of the cream solid side. Turn the heart right side out through slit; hand-stitch the opening closed and press. Center the heart in the center square of the quilt block; pin. Hand-stitch the heart in place to finish. ❖

Heart Pattern

A
Cut 1 cream solid, 16 light green floral, 28
dark rose floral & 36 dark green floral

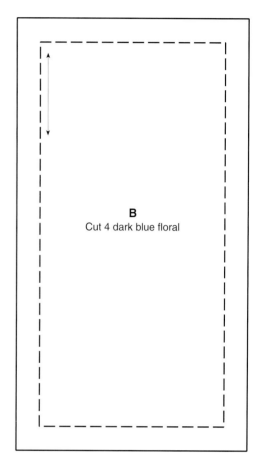

B
Cut 4 dark blue floral

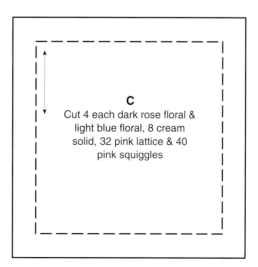

C
Cut 4 each dark rose floral &
light blue floral, 8 cream
solid, 32 pink lattice & 40
pink squiggles

Medallion Flower Quilt

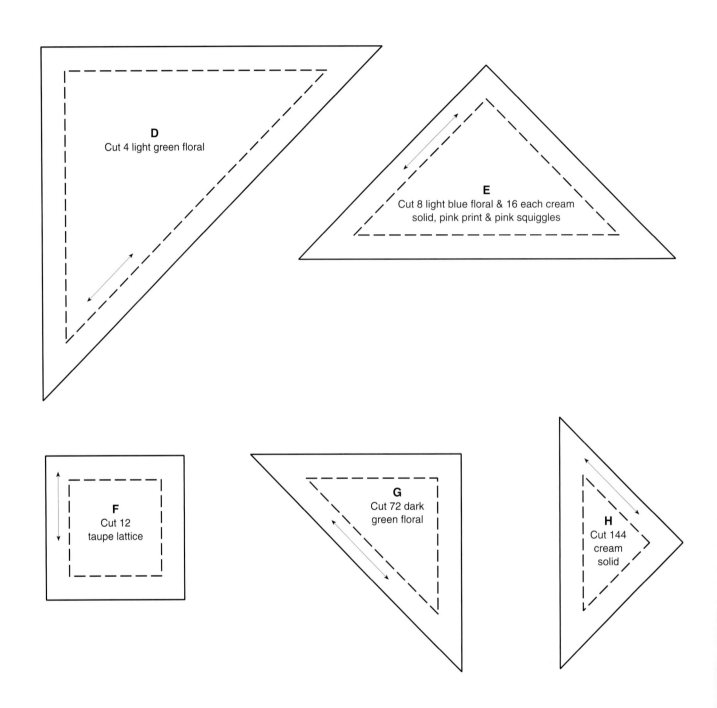

D
Cut 4 light green floral

E
Cut 8 light blue floral & 16 each cream
solid, pink print & pink squiggles

F
Cut 12
taupe lattice

G
Cut 72 dark
green floral

H
Cut 144
cream
solid

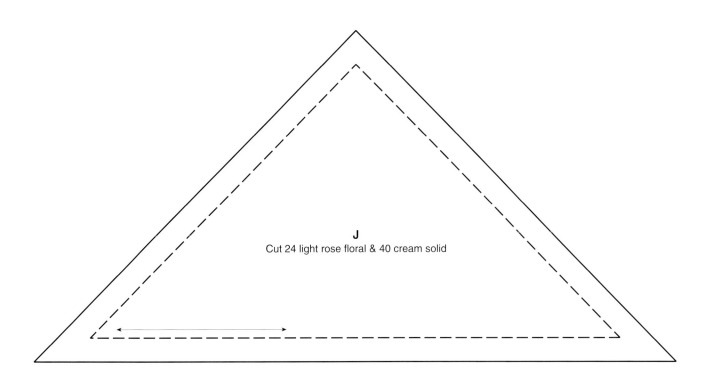

J
Cut 24 light rose floral & 40 cream solid

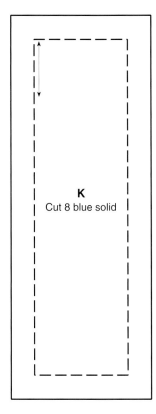

K
Cut 8 blue solid

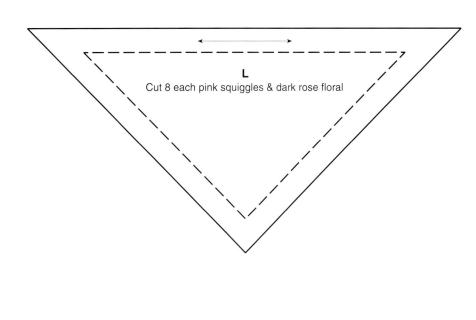

L
Cut 8 each pink squiggles & dark rose floral

Pinwheels in Squares

BY JUDITH SANDSTROM

This quilt, while made with one of the most basic and easy-to-piece quilt shapes—the pinwheel—has a special charm as a scrap quilt. Here the pinwheels are made of eight different pastel prints with a navy solid fabric holding each of the pinwheel blocks together. Alternating the pieced blocks with plain blocks makes this large quilt quick to stitch especially if you follow the quick-piecing methods given here.

Pinwheels in Squares

4 1/2" x 81 1/2"

4 1/2" x 87"

Pinwheels in Squares
Placement Diagram
81 1/2" x 96"

Pinwheels in Squares

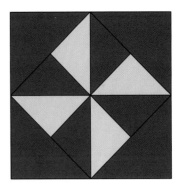

Pinwheel in a Square
10 1/4" x 10 1/4" Block

Project Specifications

Quilt Size: 81½" x 96"

Block Size: 10¼" x 10¼"

Number of Blocks: 30

Fabric & Batting

- ¼ yard each 8 pastel prints
- 2½ yards large floral print
- 2½ yards navy solid
- 3⅛ yards tan-on-tan print
- Backing 86" x 100"
- Batting 86" x 100"
- 10½ yards self-made or purchased binding

Supplies & Tools

- Tan all-purpose thread
- Basic sewing tools and supplies, rotary cutter, ruler and cutting mat

Instructions

1. Cut nine strips navy solid 6" by fabric width. Cut each strip into 6" square segments. Cut each square in half on one diagonal to make A triangles; you will need 120 A triangles.

2. Cut seven strips each navy solid and one strip each from the eight pastel prints 4½" by fabric width. Cut each strip into 4½" square segments.

Cut each square in half on one diagonal to make B triangles. You will need 120 navy solid and 30 sets of four same-pastel print B triangles.

3. Cut seven strips tan-on-tan print 10¾" by fabric width. Cut each strip into 10¾" square segments for plain blocks. You will need 20 plain blocks.

4. Cut five squares tan-on-tan print 15¾" x 15¾". Cut each square in half on both diagonals to make C triangles; you will need 18 C triangles.

5. Cut two squares tan-on-tan print 8⅛" x 8⅛". Cut each square in half on one diagonal to make D triangles. You will need four D triangles.

6. Sew a pastel print B triangle to a navy solid B triangle as shown in Figure 1; repeat for all B triangles.

Figure 1
Sew a pastel print B triangle
to a navy solid B triangle.

Pinwheels in Squares

7. Join four same-fabric B triangle units as shown in Figure 2; repeat for all B triangle units.

Figure 2
Join 4 same-fabric
B triangle units.

8. Sew an A triangle to each side of a B triangle unit as shown in Figure 3 to complete one block; repeat for 30 blocks. Press all blocks.

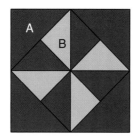

Figure 3
Sew an A triangle to each
side of a B triangle unit as
shown in Figure 3 to
complete 1 block.

Figure 4
Arrange blocks in diagonal
rows with plain squares and
C and D triangles as shown.

9. Arrange blocks in diagonal rows with plain squares and C and D triangles as shown in Figure 4; join in diagonal rows. Press seams in one direction. Join rows and add D corner triangles to opposite corners to complete the pieced center; press seams in one direction.

10. Cut two strips each large border print 5" x 82" and 5" x 87½" along length of fabric. Sew the longer strips to opposite long sides and shorter strips to the top and bottom; press seams toward strips.

11. Sandwich batting between completed top and prepared backing piece. Pin or baste layers together to hold flat.

12. Quilt as desired by hand or machine. *Note: The quilt shown was machine-quilted through the centers of each pieced and plain block and in the ditch of block and border seams using tan all-purpose thread. When quilting is complete, remove pins or basting; trim edges even.*

13. Bind edges with self-made or purchased binding to finish. ❖

Flying Geese Medallion Quilt

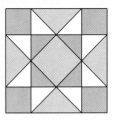

Variable Star
8" x 8" Block

BY SANDRA L. HATCH

The quilt in the photograph is actually an antique quilt, proving that making quilts from scraps goes back a long way. If you have scraps of light, medium and dark prints and shirting fabrics, you can make a quilt following these instructions. However, several fabric manufacturers today are selling reproduction fabrics adapted from old quilts, so you might prefer to re-create this quilt with those new fabrics. The quilt itself is a basic medallion quilt with a Variable Star center and borders of Flying Geese.

Flying Geese Medallion Quilt

Project Specifications
Quilt Size: 57⅝" x 65⅝"
Block Size: 8" x 8"
Number of Blocks: 1

Fabric & Batting
- Scraps of light, medium and dark prints, and shirting fabrics for flying geese units
- ⅛ yard pink solid
- ⅓ yard blue solid
- ¾ yard red print
- 1¼ yards blue print
- 1¾ yards pink print
- Backing 62" x 70"
- Batting 62" x 70"
- 7½ yards self-made or purchased binding

Supplies & Tools
- Neutral color all-purpose thread
- White quilting thread
- Basic sewing tools and supplies, rotary cutter, ruler and cutting mat

Instructions
1. To piece one center block, cut two squares blue

solid 2⅞" x 2⅞". Cut each square on one diagonal to make four A triangles.

2. Cut one square medium print 3⁵⁄₁₆" x 3⁵⁄₁₆" for B. Sew an A triangle to each side of the B square.

3. Cut eight 2½" x 2½" squares light print for C and four 2½" x 4½" rectangles medium print for D.

4. Place a C square on one corner of D; sew on one diagonal as shown in Figure 1; trim seam beyond stitching to ¼" as shown in Figure 2 and press. Place a second C square on D and sew on one diagonal as shown in Figure 3; trim and press to complete one Flying Geese unit. Repeat for four same-fabric units.

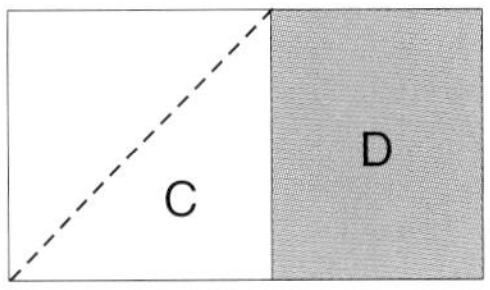

5. Cut four squares 2½" x 2½" blue solid for E.

6. Join pieced units as shown in Figure 4 to complete the center Variable Star block.

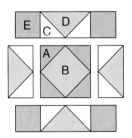

Figure 4
Join pieced units as shown
to complete the center
Variable Star block.

7. Cut four squares pink print 1½" x 1½" and four strips blue print 1½" x 8½". Sew a strip to opposite sides of the pieced block; press seams toward strips. Sew a square to each end of the remaining two strips; sew to remaining sides of the pieced block as shown in Figure 5; press seams toward strips.

Figure 1
Place a C square on 1 corner
of D; sew on 1 diagonal.

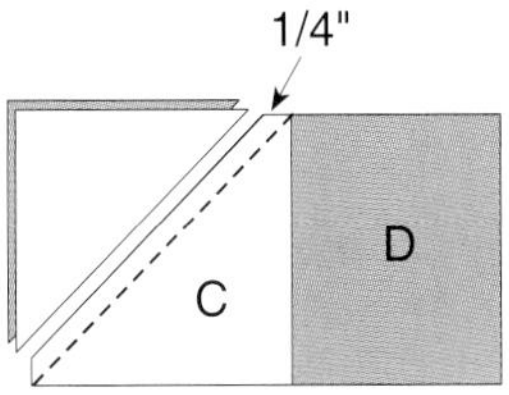

Figure 2
Trim seam beyond
stitching to 1/4".

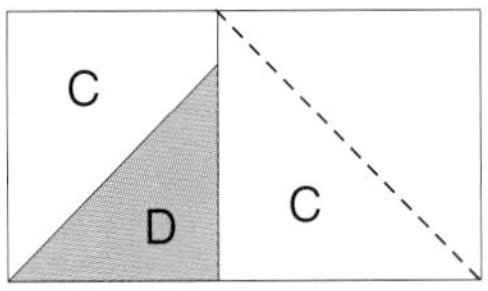

Figure 3
Place a second C square on
D and sew on 1 diagonal.

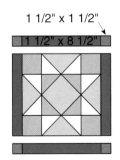

1 1/2" x 1 1/2"

1 1/2" x 8 1/2"

Figure 5
Sew a square to each end
of the remaining 2 strips;
sew to remaining sides of
the pieced block.

Flying Geese Medallion Quilt

4" x 57 5/8"

2" x 53 5/8"

Flying Geese Medallion Quilt
Placement Diagram
57 5/8" x 65 5/8"

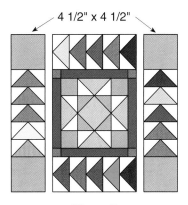

Figure 7
Sew these strips to the remaining
sides of the pieced section.

8. Cut 220 dark and medium print 2½" x 4½" rectangles for D and 440 light print 2½" x 2½" squares for C.

9. Complete 220 Flying Geese units as in step 4.

10. Join five Flying Geese units to make a geese strip as shown in Figure 6; repeat for four geese strips. Sew a geese strip to two opposite sides of the pieced center; press seams toward blue print strips.

Figure 6
Join 5 Flying Geese units
to make a geese strip.

11. Cut four 4½" x 4½" squares blue solid. Sew a square to each end of the two remaining geese strips. Sew these strips to the remaining sides of the pieced section as shown in Figure 7; press seams toward blue print strips.

12. Cut eight strips blue print 1½" x 18½", four strips red print 1½" x 18½" and four squares pink solid 3½" x 3½".

13. Sew a red print strip between two blue print strips with right sides together along length; press seams in one direction. Repeat for four strip sets.

14. Sew a strip set to opposite sides of the pieced section; press seams toward strip set. Sew a 3½" x 3½" pink solid square to each end of the remaining two strip sets. Sew to the remaining sides of the pieced section as shown in Figure 8; press seams toward strip sets.

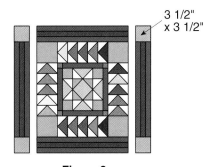

Figure 8
Sew pieced strip to the
remaining sides of the
pieced section.

15. Join 12 Flying Geese units to make a geese strip; press. Repeat for four geese strips. Cut four squares blue solid 4½" x 4½". Sew geese strips to the pieced sections and squares to geese strips as in step 10 and 11; press.

Flying Geese Medallion Quilt

16. Cut eight strips blue print and four strips red print 1½" x 32½" and four squares pink solid 3½" x 3½".

17. Sew strips together and sew to pieced section with squares as in steps 13 and 14.

18. Join 19 Flying Geese units to make a geese strip; press. Repeat for four geese strips.

19. Sew a geese strip to opposite sides of the pieced section; press seams toward strip sets. Center and sew a geese strip on remaining sides, stopping stitching at ends of the geese strips as shown in Figure 9. *Note: Do not worry about the excess at sides at this time.*

Figure 9
Stop stitching at ends of geese strips.

20. Cut eight strips blue print and four strips red print 1½" x 38½". Sew strips together as in step 13.

21. Sew a strip set to pieced section, sewing all the way to the end of the previous geese strip; press seams toward strip set.

22. Join 13 Flying Geese units to make a geese strip; press. Repeat for four strips units. Center and sew a geese strip to the pieced section, stopping stitching at ends of the geese strips as in step 19; press seams toward pieced section.

23. Cut eight strips blue print and four strips red print 1½" x 26½". Sew strips together as in step 13 and sew to pieced section as in step 21.

24. Join six Flying Geese units to make a geese strip; press. Repeat for four geese strips. Center and sew to pieced section as in step 19.

25. Cut eight strips blue print and four strips red print 1½" x 12½". Sew strips together as in step 13 and sew to pieced section as in step 21.

26. Trim excess geese strips and strip sets ¼" from point of the pink solid squares in the center of each side as shown in Figure 10. The pieced center should measure approximately 54⅛" if stitching is accurate.

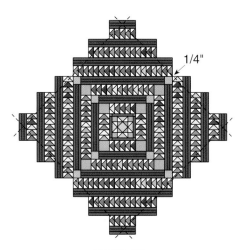

1/4"

Figure 10
Trim excess geese strips and
strip sets 1/4" from point of the
pink solid squares in the center
of each side as shown.

27. Cut two strips each pink print 2½" x 54⅛" and 4½" x 58⅛" from fabric length. Sew the shorter

strips to opposite sides and longer strips to the top and bottom of the pieced center; press seams toward strips. *Note: Check the size of your finished quilt center before cutting the border strips. Because the edge pieces are on the bias, it might stretch a little. Be careful when stitching border strips on, pin to ends and center and work to keep the piece straight when stitching.*

28. Sandwich batting between completed top and prepared backing piece; pin or baste layers together.

29. Quilt as desired by hand or machine. *Note: The sample shown was hand-quilted with white quilting thread in chain design in geese strips and a clover design in solid squares.*

30. When quilting is complete, trim edges even. Remove pins or basting. Bind edges with self-made or purchased narrow binding to finish. ❖

Indian Hatchet Patches

BY DOREEN BURBANK

This quilt designer was playing around with variations on the Indian Hatchet block (combining it with the Four-Patch block, for instance). The basic block is combined in groups of four making either X's or O's. The setting in this quilt alternates rows of X's and O's. Other settings, such as the one shown here in the alternate setting, will alter the effect.

Indian Hatchet Patches

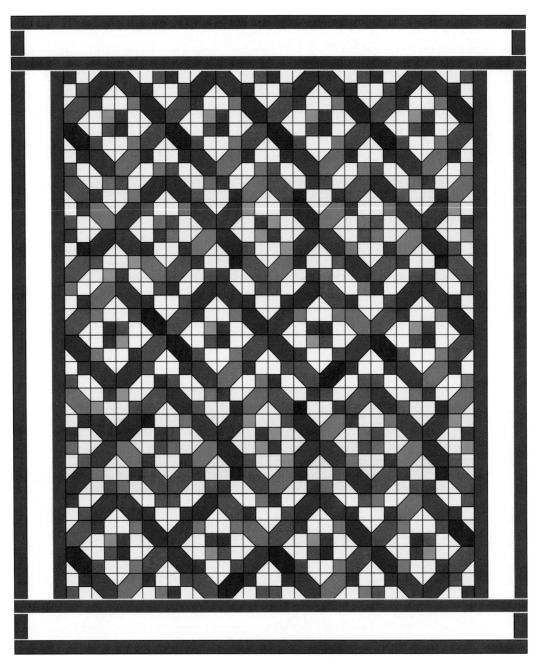

Indian Hatchet Patches
Placement Diagram
80" x 96"

Indian Hatchet Patches

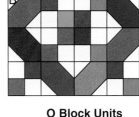

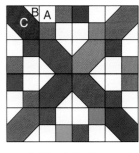

Indian Hatchet Patches
16" x 16"

O Block Units
16" x 16"
Make 12

X Block Units
16" x 16"
Make 8

Project Specifications

Quilt Size: 80" x 96"

Block Size: 8" x 8"

Number of Blocks: 80

Fabric & Batting

- 1 yard light for inner border
- 2 yards dark for borders and binding
- 3 yards dark scraps
- 3 yards light scraps
- Backing 84" x 100"
- Batting 84" x 100"
- 10 yards self-made or purchased binding

Supplies & Tools

- 2 spools all-purpose thread to match background
- Basic sewing supplies and tools

Instructions

1. Prepare templates using pattern pieces given. Cut as directed on each piece to complete 80 blocks.

2. Cut and piece border strips as shown in Figure 1 to make a total of about 330" of combined strip border as shown in Figure 2 as follows: Cut and

construct a strip 4½" by approximately 330" from light fabric; cut and construct two strips 2½" wide by approximately 330" from dark fabric.

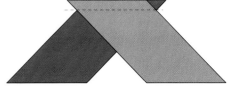

Figure 1
Piece ends of strips together
at an angle as shown.

2 1/2"
4 1/2"
2 1/2"

Figure 2
Join strips to make border strip.

3. To piece one block, sew two dark and two light A pieces together; repeat. Join the two units to make a Four-Patch; repeat and press units.

4. Sew B to C to B; repeat and press. Join the B-C units with the A units referring to Figure 3; repeat for 80 blocks.

Indian Hatchet Patches

5. Arrange four blocks and join as shown in Figure 4 to make X units; repeat for eight X units. Press all units.

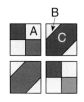

Figure 3
Join A units with B-C
units to make 1 block.

Figure 4
Arrange 4 blocks to
make X units.

6. Arrange four blocks and join as shown in Figure 5 to make O units; repeat for 12 O units. Press all units.

Figure 5
Arrange 4 blocks
to make O units.

7. Arrange the X and O units in rows as shown in Figure 6 to make quilt top. Join units in rows; join rows to complete quilt center and press.

8. Sew the pieced border strip to one side; trim off even with quilt center. Repeat for opposite side and then top and bottom; press.

Figure 6
Arrange X and O units in rows.

9. If desired, a filler piece cut 2½" x 4½" may be appliquéd to each end of the top and bottom border pieces to give a more finished appearance to border corners. Compare the two different corners in Figure 7.

10. Sandwich batting between completed top and prepared backing piece. Baste or pin layers together.

11. Quilt as desired by hand or machine. When quilting is complete, trim edges even.

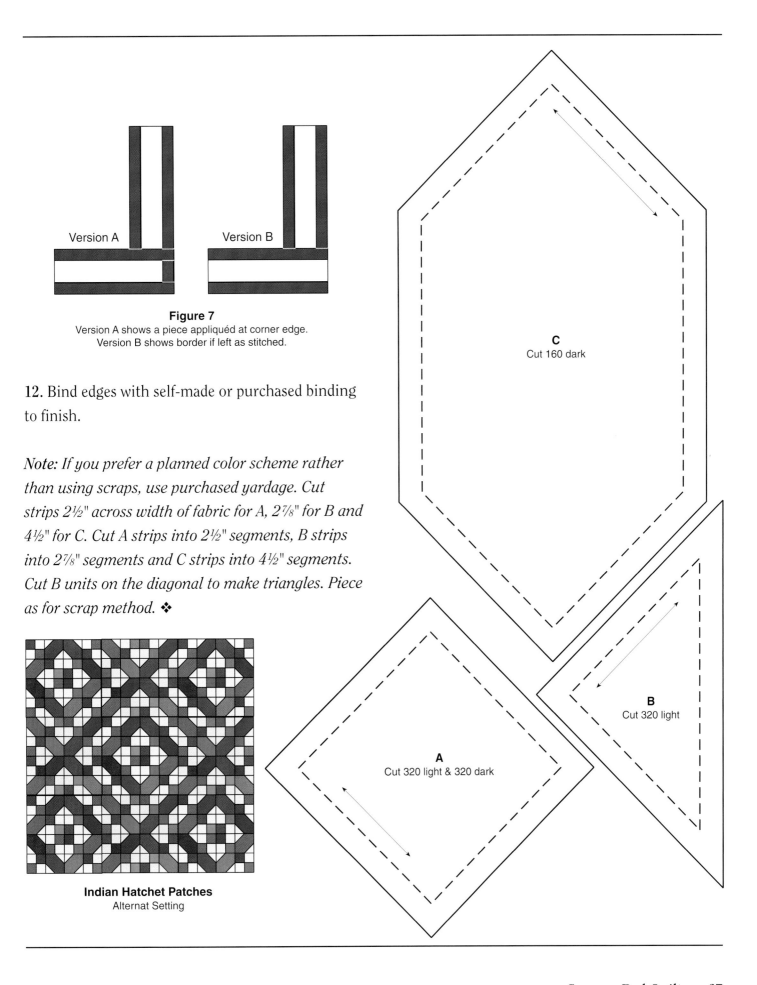

Figure 7
Version A shows a piece appliquéd at corner edge.
Version B shows border if left as stitched.

12. Bind edges with self-made or purchased binding to finish.

Note: If you prefer a planned color scheme rather than using scraps, use purchased yardage. Cut strips 2½" across width of fabric for A, 2⅞" for B and 4½" for C. Cut A strips into 2½" segments, B strips into 2⅞" segments and C strips into 4½" segments. Cut B units on the diagonal to make triangles. Piece as for scrap method. ❖

Version A

Version B

C
Cut 160 dark

B
Cut 320 light

A
Cut 320 light & 320 dark

Indian Hatchet Patches
Alternat Setting

Vice President's Quilt

BY RUTH M. SWASEY

A long time ago someone had the idea to name a quilt in honor of the Vice President, and here's a modern version that would certainly honor an important person in your life. Scraps of dark and light fabrics are used to create the blocks that are then joined with blue print and rose print sashing strips. This is a true scrap quilt because as many as 60 different fabrics could be used to create the blocks, or you could decide to make use of the same light and dark fabric.

Vice President's Quilt

Vice President's Quilt
Placement Diagram
78" x 93"

Vice President's Quilt

Project Specifications

Quilt Size: 78" x 93"
Block Size: 12" x 12" and 3" x 3"
Number of Blocks: 30 large; 42 small

Fabric & Batting

- 1½ yards light rose print
- 2 yards total light print
- 2½ yards dark blue print
- 4 yards total dark print scraps
- Backing 82" x 97"
- Batting 82" x 97"
- 10 yards self-made or purchased binding

Supplies & Tools

- Neutral color all-purpose thread
- White quilting thread
- Basic sewing tools and supplies, rotary cutter, ruler and cutting mat

Instructions

1. Prepare templates using pattern pieces given; cut as directed on each piece for one block.

2. Cut two squares dark print scrap 4⅞" x 4⅞" for D. *Note: Use the same dark print scraps for pieces A and D and the same light print scraps for pieces*

Vice President
12" x 12" Block

B and C. Cut each square in half on one diagonal to make D triangles.

3. Join four A pieces with B as shown in Figure 1.

4. Sew C to D; repeat for four units. Sew a C-D unit to each side of the A-B unit to complete one block as shown in Figure 2; repeat for 30 blocks.

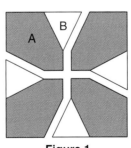

Figure 1
Join 4 A pieces with B.

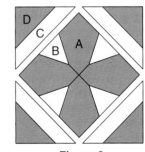

Figure 2
Sew a C-D unit to each side of the A-B unit to complete 1 block.

5. Cut 24 strips light rose print and 48 strips dark blue print 1½" by fabric width.

Vice President's Quilt

6. Sew a light rose print strip between two dark blue print strips with right sides together along length; press seams toward dark blue print strips. Repeat for 24 strip sets.

7. Subcut strip sets into 12½" segments as shown in Figure 3; repeat for 71 segments for sashing strips.

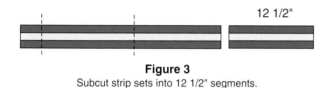

Figure 3
Subcut strip sets into 12 1/2" segments.

8. Cut seven strips dark blue print and eight strips light rose print 1½" by fabric width.

9. Sew a light rose print strip between two dark blue print strips with right sides together along length; press seams toward dark blue print strips. Repeat for two strip sets.

10. Subcut strip sets into 1½" segments as shown in Figure 4; repeat for 42 segments.

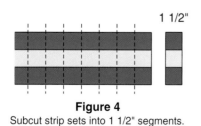

Figure 4
Subcut strip sets into 1 1/2" segments.

11. Sew a dark blue print strip between two light rose print strips with right sides together along length; press seams toward dark blue print strip. Repeat for three strip sets.

12. Subcut strip sets into 1½" segments as shown in Figure 5; repeat for 84 segments.

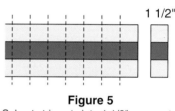

Figure 5
Subcut strip sets into 1 1/2" segments.

13. Join two light/dark/light segments with one dark/light/dark segment to make a Nine-Patch sashing block as shown in Figure 6; repeat for 42 sashing blocks.

Figure 6
Join 2 light/dark/light segments with 1 dark/light/dark segment to make a Nine-Patch sashing block.

14. Join five blocks with six sashing strips to make a block row as shown in Figure 7; repeat for six block rows. Press seams toward sashing strips.

Figure 7
Join 5 blocks with 6 sashing strips to make a block row.

15. Join six sashing blocks with five sashing strips to make a sashing row as shown in Figure 8; repeat for seven sashing rows.

Figure 8
Join 6 sashing blocks with 5 sashing strips to make a sashing row.

16. Join sashing rows with block rows to complete quilt top referring to the Placement Diagram. Press seams in one direction.

17. Sandwich batting between completed top and prepared backing piece; pin or baste layers together to hold flat.

18. Hand-quilt in the ditch of seams and as desired using white quilting thread.

19. When quilting is complete, remove pins or basting. Bind edges with self-made or purchased binding to finish. ❖

Vice President's Quilt

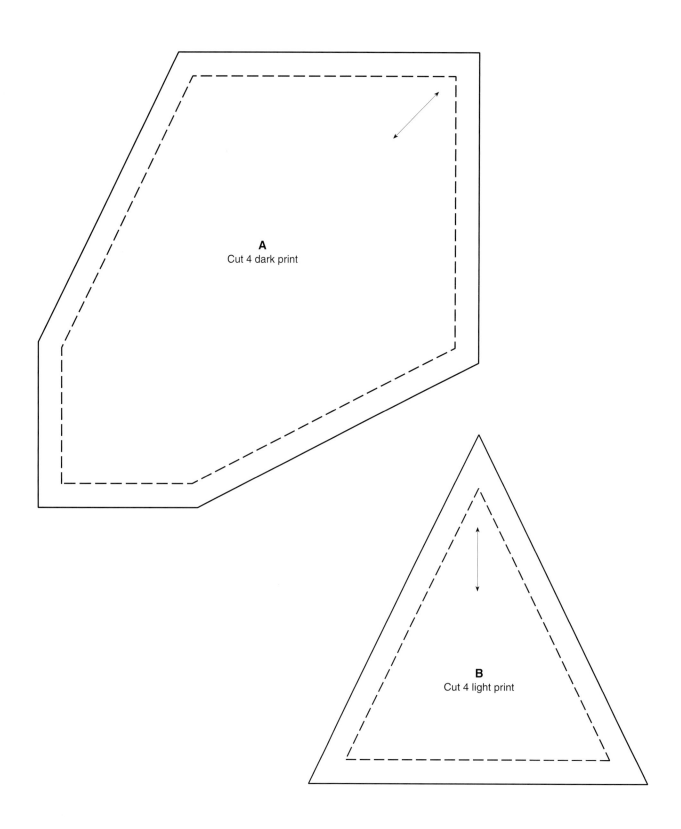

A
Cut 4 dark print

B
Cut 4 light print

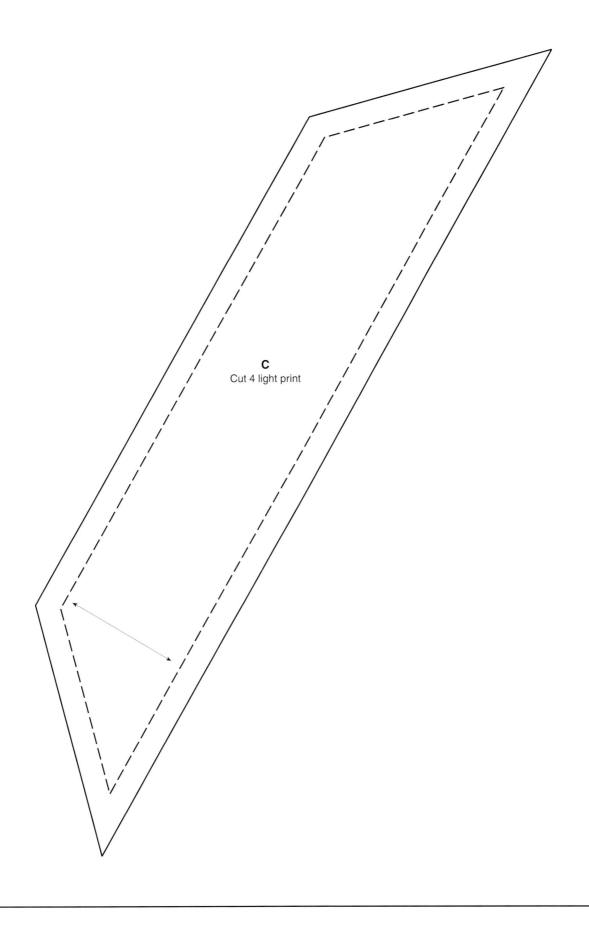

C
Cut 4 light print

Nine-Patch Scrap Quilt

BY LUCY A. FAZELY

With 180 different-colored blocks, this is truly a scrap quilt! Whether you have that many fabrics in your stash, or you choose to purchase fabrics, remember to use a diverse selection of colors in prints and solids to keep your quilt bright and exciting. In this quilt, each scrap fabric will need to make four or five 2½" squares for each block. Don't be afraid to use bright and colorful fabrics, as well as dull fabrics, and large and small prints too. If you prefer, you can use similar fabric scraps mixed in one block. Just try to keep them about the same color, shade and of similar prints.

Nine Patch Scrap Quilt

Nine-Patch Scrap Quilt
Placement Diagram
72" x 90"

Nine-Patch Scrap Quilt

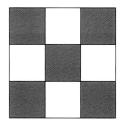 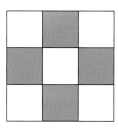

Nine-Patch
6" x 6" Block

Nine-Patch
6" x 6" Block

Project Specifications

Quilt Size: 72" x 90"

Block Size: 6" x 6"

Number of Blocks: 180

Fabric & Batting

- Scraps of fabric to equal 3¾ yards
- 3¾ yards white solid
- Backing 76" x 94"
- Batting 76" x 94"
- 10½ yards self-made or purchased binding

Supplies & Tools

- Neutral color all-purpose thread
- Basic sewing supplies and tools

Instructions

1. Cut 51 strips white 2½" by fabric width. Cut strips into 810 squares 2½" x 2½". *Note: If you prefer to work with strips, cut one strip each of several different light and dark fabrics. Sew the strips together in the order shown in the rows shown in Figures 1 and 2. Cut strip sets apart in 2½" segments. Join the segments to make blocks, again referring to Figures 1 and 2.*

2. Cut fabric scraps into a total of 810 squares

2½" x 2½". You will need 90 sets of four squares and 90 sets of five squares.

3. Join squares to make a block as shown in Figure 1; repeat for 90 blocks. Join squares to make a block as shown in Figure 2; repeat for 90 blocks.

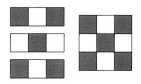 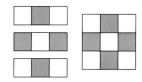

Figure 1
Make a Nine-Patch as shown.

Figure 2
Make a Nine-Patch as shown.

4. Lay the blocks out in 15 rows of 12 blocks each, placing darker blocks next to lighter blocks.

5. Stitch blocks together in rows; stitch rows together to make pieced top. Press row seams in one direction.

6. Sandwich batting between completed top and prepared backing piece. Baste layers together to hold flat.

7. Quilt by hand or machine, or tie quilt layers to hold together.

8. When quilting is complete, trim edges even. Bind edges with self-made or purchased binding. ❖

Prairie Claw

BY JODI BARROWS

Red, black and gold scraps—whether they are prints, plaids or checks—combine to make this scrap quilt a coordinated whole. Because the design calls for 28 plain blocks, there is lots of room for fine quilting in the plain blocks. The leaf pattern given here would look spectacular with the Prairie Claw blocks. This quiltmaker quilted the blocks with black quilting thread, which made the quilting stitches stand out.

Prairie Claw

Prairie Claw
Placement Diagram
87 1/2" x 99"

Prairie Claw

Prairie Claw
11 1/2" x 11 1/2" Block

Project Specifications

Quilt Size: 87½" x 99"

Block Size: 11½" x 11½"

Number of Blocks: 28 pieced; 28 plain

Fabric & Batting

- Scraps red, black and gold prints, plaids and checks
- 1¼ yards red check
- 5 yards cream solid
- Backing 92" x 103"
- Batting 92" x 103"
- 10¾ yards self-made or purchased binding

Figure 1
Sew B to each side
of A as shown.

Supplies & Tools

- All-purpose thread to match fabrics
- Black quilting thread
- Basic sewing tools and supplies and water-erasable marker or pen

Instructions

1. Prepare templates using pattern pieces given. Cut as directed on each piece for one block; repeat for 28 blocks.

2. Sew B to each side of A as shown in Figure 1; repeat for five units.

3. Join the A-B units with C to make rows as shown in Figure 2; join rows to complete block center.

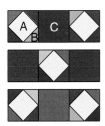

Figure 2
Join the A-B units with
C to make rows.

4. Sew B to each short side of E as shown in Figure 3; repeat for four units.

Prairie Claw

Figure 3
Sew B to each
short side of E.

5. Sew D to each B end of a B-E unit as shown in Figure 4; repeat for four units.

6. Sew F to each end of two D-B-E units as shown in Figure 5.

Figure 4
Sew D to each B
end of a B-E unit.

Figure 5
Sew F to each end of 2 D-B-E units.

7. Arrange pieced units with block center as shown in Figure 6; join to complete one block and press. Repeat for 28 blocks.

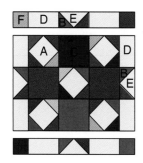

Figure 6
Arrange pieced units with block center.

8. Cut 28 squares cream solid 12" x 12".

9. Arrange four pieced blocks with three cream solid squares to make a row as shown in Figure 7; repeat for four rows. Press seams in one direction.

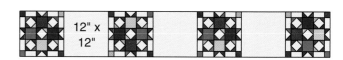

Figure 7
Arrange 4 pieced blocks with 3 cream solid
squares to make a row as shown.

10. Arrange three pieced blocks with four cream solid squares to make a row as shown in Figure 8; repeat for four rows. Press seams in one direction.

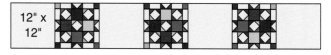

Figure 8
Arrange 3 pieced blocks with 4 cream
solid squares to make a row.

11. Join rows referring to the Placement Diagram to complete quilt center; press seams in one direction.

12. Cut and piece two strips each 4" x 88" and 4" x 92½" red check. Sew the longer strips to opposite sides and shorter strips to the top and bottom; press seams toward strips.

13. Using water-erasable marker or pen, mark the leaf quilting design given on the cream solid squares referring to Figure 9. Mark the ribbon quilting design on the border strips.

Figure 9
Mark the quilting design given on the cream solid squares.

14. Sandwich batting between completed top and prepared backing; pin or baste layers together to hold flat.

15. Quilt on marked lines by hand or machine using black quilting thread. When quilting is complete, trim excess batting and backing; remove pins or basting.

16. Bind edges with self-made or purchased binding to finish. ❖

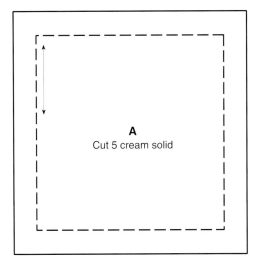

A
Cut 5 cream solid

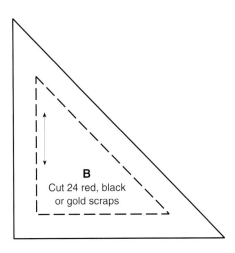

B
Cut 24 red, black or gold scraps

Prairie Claw

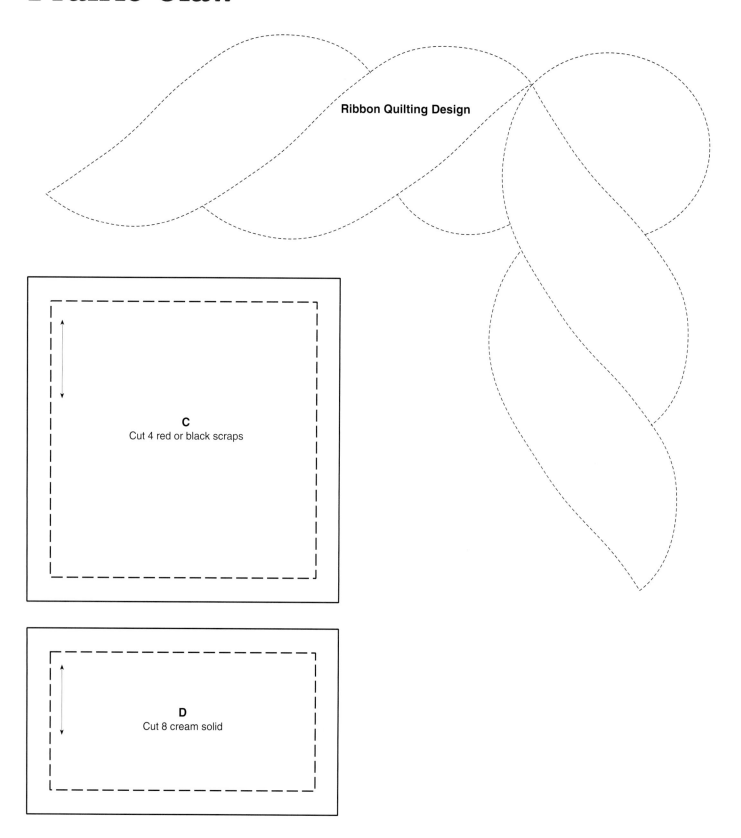

Ribbon Quilting Design

C
Cut 4 red or black scraps

D
Cut 8 cream solid

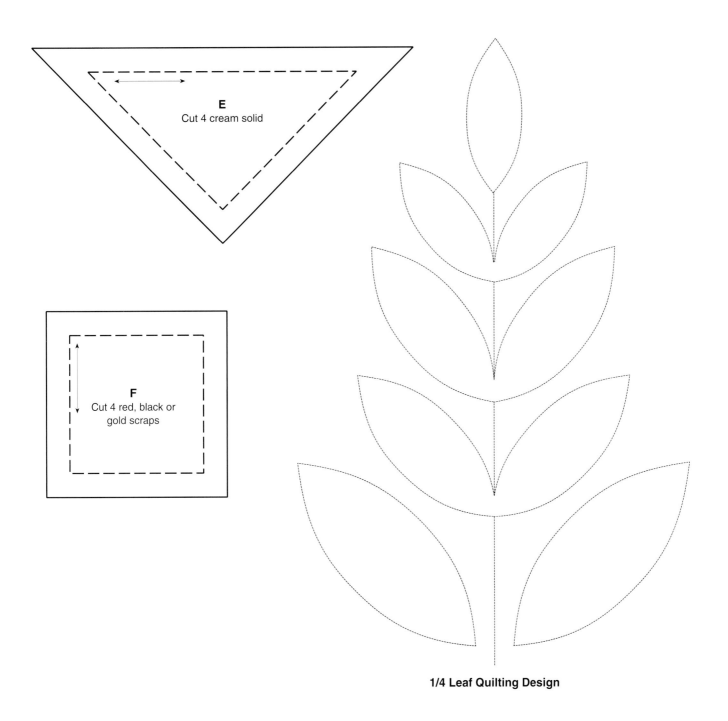

E
Cut 4 cream solid

F
Cut 4 red, black or
gold scraps

1/4 Leaf Quilting Design

Am I Blue?

BY HOLLY DANIELS

If you have a stash of blue fabrics, you can quickly turn them into a bed-size quilt using these quick-piecing methods. While each of the blocks in this quilt is constructed in the same manner, the blocks can vary if you use different fabrics for each block.

Am I Blue?

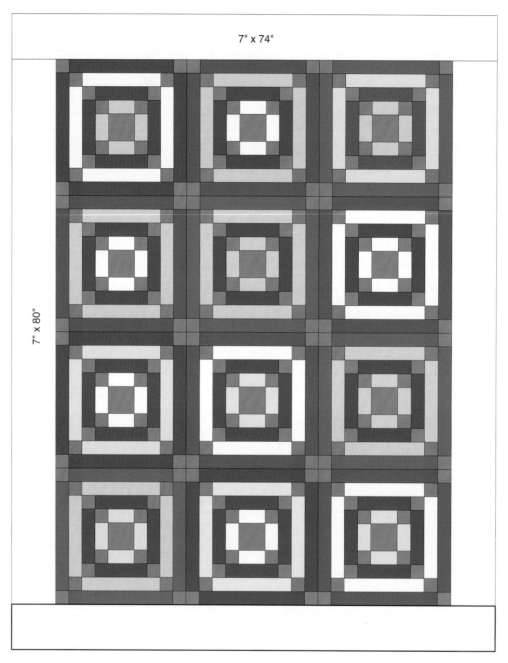

7" x 74"

7" x 80"

Am I Blue?
Placement Diagram
74" x 94"

Am I Blue?

Project Specifications

Quilt Size: 74" x 94"

Block Size: 20" x 20"

Number of Blocks: 12

Fabric & Batting

- 1¼ yards blue solid
- 1¾ yards blue-and-white print
- 2 yards total dark blue prints
- 3 yards total light blue prints
- Backing 78" x 98"
- Batting 78" x 98"
- 9¾ yards self-made or purchased binding

Supplies & Tools

- Neutral color all-purpose thread
- Clear nylon monofilament
- Basic sewing supplies and tools, rotary cutter, ruler and cutting mat

Instructions

1. Cut the following pieces for each block: four rectangles each 2½" x 4½" (C) and 2½" x 12½" (E) light blue prints, and four rectangles each 2½" x 8½" (D) and 2½" x 16½" (F) dark blue prints. Repeat for 12 blocks. *Note: One 2½" by fabric width strip will yield about nine 4½" pieces, four or five 8½" pieces, three 12" pieces or two 16½" pieces.*

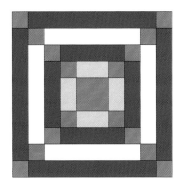

Am I Blue?
20" x 20" Block

2. Cut two 4½" by fabric width strips and twelve 2½" by fabric width strips blue solid. Subcut the 4½" strips into 4½" segments for A; you will need 12 A squares. Subcut the 2½" strips into 2½" segments for B; you will need 192 B squares.

3. Arrange all pieces on a flat surface from shortest to longest.

4. Sew two C pieces to each side of A; sew B to each end of two more C pieces and sew to the A-C unit to complete the block center referring to Figure 1. Press seams away from A. *Note: One block uses same-fabric C, D, E and F pieces; no blocks are identical.*

Figure 1
Sew 2 C pieces to each side of A; sew B to each end of 2 more C pieces and sew to the A-C unit to complete the block center.

Am I Blue?

5. Sew two D pieces to opposite sides of the A-C-B unit; sew B to each end of two more D pieces and sew to the A-C-B-D unit referring to Figure 2.

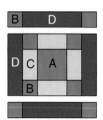

Figure 2
Sew 2 D pieces to opposite sides of the A-C-B unit; sew B to each end of 2 more D pieces and sew to the A-C-B-D unit.

6. Continue sewing B, E and F pieces to the previously pieced unit until the block is complete as shown in Figure 3. Repeat for 12 blocks.

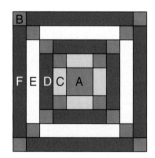

Figure 3
Continue sewing B, E and F pieces to the previously pieced unit until the block is complete.

7. Arrange the blocks in four rows of three blocks each. When you are satisfied with the arrangement, join three blocks to make a row; repeat for four rows. Press seams in one direction.

8. Join the rows to complete the pieced center; press seams in one direction.

9. Cut and piece two strips each 7½" x 80½" and 7½" x 74½" blue-and-white print. Sew the longer strips to opposite long sides of the pieced center and the shorter strips to the top and bottom; press seams toward strips.

10. Sandwich batting between completed top and prepared backing; pin or baste layers together to hold flat.

11. Quilt as desired by hand or machine. *Note: The quilt shown was machine-quilted with an X through each block and diagonal lines between these lines as shown in Figure 4, using clear nylon monofilament in the top of the machine and all-purpose thread in the bobbin.*

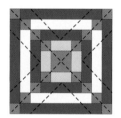

Figure 4
Quilt each block as shown.

12. When quilting is complete, trim edges even and remove pins or basting. Bind edges with self-made or purchased binding to finish. ❖

Atlantis

BY CONNIE RAND

Finding fabrics with undersea designs prompted this quilter to come up with a quilt that would reflect the movement and colors of the ocean. If you don't have scraps of fabrics with fish themes, you can still make this lovely quilt by using other prints and solids. The quilt may look complicated and difficult to sew, but with these quick-piecing methods, your quilt can be completed before your ship docks.

Atlantis

Project Specifications

Quilt Size: 44" x 52"

Fabric & Batting

- ¼ yard each scallop and light and dark seaweed prints
- ½ yard each abalone, anemone, fish scale and nautilus prints
- 1¾ yards fish tail print
- Backing 48" x 56"
- Batting 48" x 56"
- 6 yards self-made or purchased binding

Supplies & Tools

- Coordinating all-purpose thread
- 1 spool silver metallic thread
- Basic sewing tools and supplies, fade-out fabric marker, rotary cutter, ruler and cutting mat

Instructions

1. Prewash and iron all fabrics.

2. Cut six strips anemone print, five strips each of abalone and nautilus prints, four strips fish scale print and two strips each scallop, fish tail and light seaweed prints 2⅞" by fabric width. Cut strips into 2⅞" x 2⅞" squares. Cut squares on one diagonal to make triangles. Sew triangles together as shown in Figure 1 and referring to the Color Key on page 96.

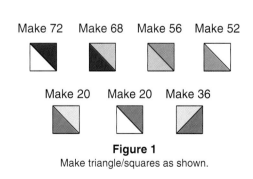

Make 72 Make 68 Make 56 Make 52

Make 20 Make 20 Make 36

Figure 1
Make triangle/squares as shown.

3. Cut two strips each light and dark seaweed prints 1½" by fabric width. Join strips with right sides together along length as shown in Figure 2; cut into 1½"-wide segments. Join two segments to make a Four-Patch unit as shown in Figure 3; repeat for 25 Four-Patch units.

Figure 2
Sew strips together as shown; cut
into 1 1/2" segments.

Make 25

Figure 3
Make Four-Patch
units as shown.

4. Cut 12 strips 1½" x 2½" anemone print. Cut four squares abalone print 1½" x 1½".

5. Join three Four-Patch units with two 1½" x 2½" abalone print strips to make a Four-Patch row as shown in Figure 4; repeat for three rows.

6. Join three 1½" x 2½" anemone print strips with two 1½" x 1½" abalone print squares to make a sashing row; repeat for two sashing rows.

7. Join Four-Patch rows and sashing rows again referring to Figure 4 to make Four-Patch center section.

1 1/2" x 2 1/2"

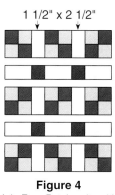

Figure 4
Join Four-Patch units with
strips and squares as shown.

8. Cut two strips abalone print and one strip each nautilus and scallop prints 1½" x 44". Join one strip each scallop and abalone prints with right sides together along length; cut into 3½"-wide segments as shown in Figure 5. Join one strip each nautilus and abalone prints along length; cut into 5½"-wide segments again referring to Figure 5.

9. Join two scallop/abalone segments with three Four-Patch units as shown in Figure 6; repeat. Join two scallop/abalone segments with one Four-Patch unit; repeat.

Atlantis

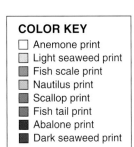

COLOR KEY
- ☐ Anemone print
- Light seaweed print
- Fish scale print
- Nautilus print
- Scallop print
- Fish tail print
- Abalone print
- Dark seaweed print

Atlantis
Placement Diagram
44" x 52"

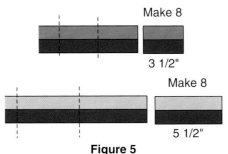

Make 8

3 1/2"

Make 8

5 1/2"

Figure 5
Cut scallop/abalone strip set into 3 1/2"
segments; cut nautilus/abalone strip
set into 5 1/2" segments.

Figure 6
Join 3 1/2" segments with
Four-Patch units as shown.

10. Join two nautilus/abalone segments with three Four-Patch units as shown in Figure 7; repeat. Join two nautilus/abalone segments with one Four-Patch unit; repeat.

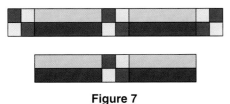

Figure 7
Join 5 1/2" segments with Four-Patch
units as shown.

11. Join segment/Four-Patch strips with Four-Patch center section as shown in Figure 8.

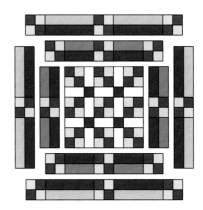

Figure 8
Join segment/Four-Patch strips with
Four-Patch center section.

12. Combine eight light seaweed/fish tail triangle/squares to make Row 1 as shown in Figure 9; repeat. Combine 10 light seaweed/fish tail triangle/squares to make Row 2 again referring to Figure 9; repeat.

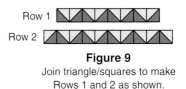

Figure 9
Join triangle/squares to make
Rows 1 and 2 as shown.

13. Combine 10 light seaweed/scallop triangle/squares to make Row 3 as shown in Figure 10; repeat.

Figure 10
Join triangle/squares to make
Row 3 as shown.

14. Combine 10 anemone/scallop triangle/squares to make Row 4 as shown in Figure 11; repeat.

Row 4

Figure 11
Join triangle/squares to make
Row 4 as shown.

15. Combine 10 anemone/fish scale triangle/squares to make Row 5 as shown in Figure 12; repeat. Combine 16 anemone/fish scale triangle/squares to make Row 6 again referring to Figure 12; repeat.

Row 5
Row 6

Figure 12
Join triangle/squares to make
Rows 5 and 6 as shown.

16. Cut four squares nautilus print 1½" x 1½". Combine 12 nautilus/fish scale triangle/squares to make Row 7 as shown in Figure 13; repeat. Combine 16 nautilus/fish scale triangle/squares with two 1½" x 1½" nautilus print squares to make Row 8 again referring to Figure 13; repeat.

Row 7
Row 8

Figure 13
Join triangle/squares to make Row 7. Join 1 1/2" squares
with triangle/squares to make Row 8.

17. Combine 14 nautilus/abalone triangle/squares to make Row 9 as shown in Figure 14; repeat. Combine 20 nautilus/abalone triangle squares to make Row 10 again referring to Figure 14; repeat.

Row 9
Row 10

Figure 14
Join triangle/squares to make Row 11. Join 1 1/2" squares
with triangle/squares to make Row 12.

18. Cut four squares anemone print 1½" x 1½". Combine 16 anemone/abalone triangle/squares to make Row 11 as shown in Figure 15; repeat. Combine 20 anemone/abalone triangle/squares with two 1½" x 1½" anemone print squares to make Row 12 again referring to Figure 15; repeat.

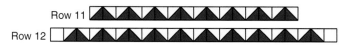

Row 11
Row 12

Figure 15
Join triangle/squares to make
Rows 11 and 12 as shown.

19. Join rows in numerical order with pieced center section as shown in Figure 16; press.

Figure 16
Join rows with pieced center section.

20. Cut four strips fish tail print 4½" x 44½". Sew two strips to opposite long sides of quilt center; press. Sew remaining strips to top and bottom; press.

21. Sandwich batting between completed top and prepared backing; pin or baste layers together to hold flat.

22. Quilt as desired by hand or machine, using silver metallic thread in the top of the machine and all-purpose thread to match backing in the bobbin.

23. When quilting is complete, trim batting and backing edges even with quilt top; remove pins or basting.

24. Bind edges with self-made or purchased binding to finish. ❖

Hugs & Kisses

BY JUDITH SANDSTROM

More than 18 different fabrics
are used to make the Hugs
& Kisses blocks in this quilt.
Three quilt blocks are made
of each color, and using quick
cutting and sewing methods,
the quilt can be put together
in little time. It will, however,
garner lots of hugs and
kisses from the happy recipient.

Hugs & Kisses

3 1/2" x 52"

3 1/2" x 74 1/2"

Hugs & Kisses
Placement Diagram
52" x 74 1/2"

Hugs & Kisses

Project Specifications
Quilt Size: 52" x 74½"
Block Size: 7½" x 7½"
Number of Blocks: 54

Fabric & Batting
- ⅛ yard each 18 different prints
- 2¼ yards stripe
- 2½ yards muslin or tone-on-tone natural color for background
- Backing 56" x 78"
- Batting 56" x 78"
- 6 yards self-made or purchased binding

Supplies & Tools
- Neutral color all-purpose thread
- 1 spool quilting thread
- Basic sewing supplies and tools, transparent ruler, rotary cutter and mat

Instructions
1. Prewash and iron all fabrics.

2. Cut 36 strips 2½" by fabric width from background fabric.

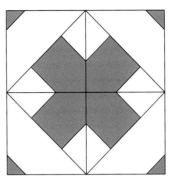

Hugs & Kisses
7 1/2" x 7 1/2" Block

3. Cut one strip 2½" by fabric width from each of the 18 varied fabrics.

4. Cut two strips 4" x 54" and two strips 4" x 78" along the straight of grain of border stripe fabric. *Note: If using nondirectional fabric, cut enough 4" by fabric width strips to piece into four border strips, two each approximately 54" and 78" long.*

5. Stitch one print strip between two muslin strips with right sides together along length; press seams open. *Note: Directions are given for making three blocks of one color. Repeat for the remaining 17 colors for a total of 54 blocks.*

6. Cut the pieced strips into six 6½" x 6½" squares. Each strip will make three 8" (includes seams) blocks.

Hugs & Kisses

7. Cut each square on both diagonals to make four right triangles as shown in Figure 1.

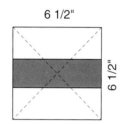

6 1/2"

6 1/2"

Figure 1
Cut segments on both
diagonals as shown.

8. Rearrange the triangles cut in step 7 to make a block as shown in Figure 2. Repeat for three blocks in each color, using all 17 fabrics for a total of 54 blocks.

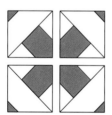

Figure 2
Arrange cut segments
to make 1 block.

9. Arrange the pieced blocks in nine rows of six blocks each and stitch. Stitch rows together; press all seams open.

10. Fold each border strip to find center. Sew shorter striped border strips to top and bottom and longer strips to opposite sides of quilt center, centering creased folds on strips to center of pieced section and mitering corners. Trim excess after stitching strips; press seams toward strips.

11. Sandwich batting between completed top and prepared backing piece. Pin or baste layers together to hold flat for quilting.

12. Hand- or machine-quilt as desired. When quilting is complete, remove pins or basting.

13. Bind edges with self-made or purchased binding to finish. ❖

Taffy

BY JANET JONES WORLEY

The pastel prints used in this quilt so reminded the designer of the many colors of taffy candy that she called the quilt Taffy. Two different blocks are combined to create the delightful design. Because the blocks can be created with simple, quick-piecing methods, the quilt can be finished in no time. Your completed quilt will surely look good enough to eat!

Taffy

Project Specifications

Quilt Size: 47" x 56½"

Block Size: 8" x 8"

Number of Blocks: 6 Square-in-a-Square; 6 Hourglass

Fabric & Batting

- ½ yard each white-on-white, yellow, aqua, blue, green and pink prints
- 1¾ yards large pink print
- Backing 51" x 61"
- Batting 51" x 61"
- 6½ yards self-made or purchased binding

Supplies & Tools

- Neutral color all-purpose thread
- Clear nylon monofilament
- Basic sewing tools and supplies, rotary cutter, ruler and cutting mat

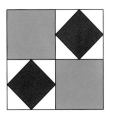

Square-in-a-Square
8" x 8" Block

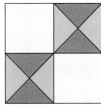

Hourglass
8" x 8" Block

Instructions

1. Cut three strips 2½" by fabric width white-on-white print; subcut into 2½" square segments for A. You will need 48 A squares.

2. Cut six squares 2" x 2" white-on-white print for B.

3. Cut two strips each 4½" by fabric width yellow, blue and green prints; subcut into 4½" square segments for D. You will need 12 D squares of each color.

4. Cut two strips each 2" by fabric width yellow, pink, aqua and large pink prints and one strip each white-on-white and green prints; subcut into 3"

segments for C. You will need 14 C segments each white-on-white and green prints and 16 C segments from other colors.

5. Cut two squares each yellow and large pink prints 3" x 3" for F.

6. Cut one strip each aqua and pink prints 5¼" by fabric width; subcut each strip into 5¼" square segments for E. You will need six each aqua and pink print E squares.

7. To piece one Square-in-a-Square block, draw a diagonal line on each white-on-white print A square. Place one A square on opposite corners of a blue print D square as shown in Figure 1; stitch on drawn diagonal lines, again referring to Figure 1.

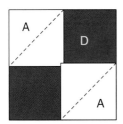

Figure 1
Place 1 A square on opposite
corners of a blue print D square;
stitch on drawn diagonal lines.

8. Trim excess beyond seam to ¼" on each A square as shown in Figure 2; press remaining triangle

section flat as shown in Figure 3. Repeat on opposite corners of the D square to make an A-D unit as shown in Figure 4. Repeat for two A-D units.

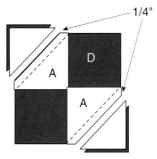

Figure 2
Trim excess beyond seam
to 1/4" on each A square.

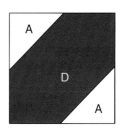

Figure 3
Press remaining
triangle section flat.

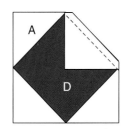

Figure 4
Repeat on opposite
corners of the D square
to make an A-D unit.

Taffy

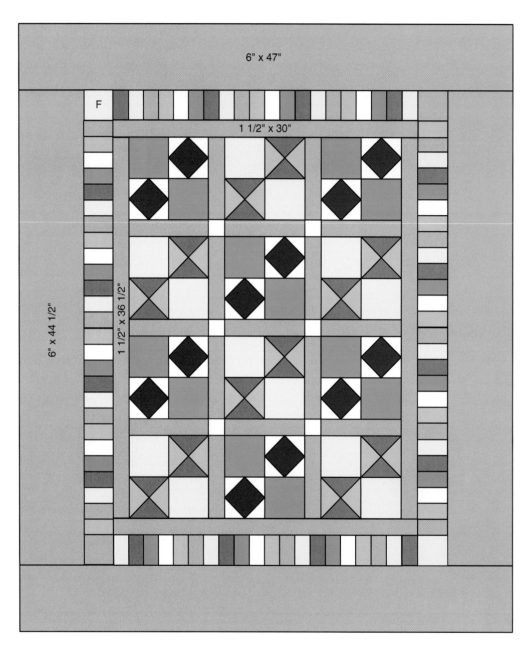

6" x 47"

F

1 1/2" x 30"

6" x 44 1/2"

1 1/2" x 36 1/2"

Taffy
Placement Diagram
47" x 56 1/2"

9. Join two A-D units with two green print D squares to complete one Square-in-a-Square block as shown in Figure 5; repeat for six blocks.

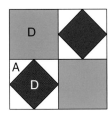

Figure 5
Join 2 A-D units with 2 green print D squares to complete 1 Square-in-a-Square block.

10. To make one Hourglass block, draw diagonal lines from corner to corner on both diagonals of each aqua and pink print E square. With right sides together, match the lines of one aqua print E to one pink print E.

11. Stitch ¼" on both sides of only one drawn line as shown in Figure 6. Cut units apart on line between stitching as shown in Figure 7. Press units open, pressing seam toward aqua print E piece to make two triangle/squares. Repeat for all pink and aqua E squares.

12. Extend the drawn line from the corner of one pink print E to the corner of one aqua print E on the wrong side of one unit as shown in Figure 8. Match both triangle/squares with contrasting fabrics facing and marked unit on top as shown in Figure 9. Stitch a ¼" seam on both sides of the marked line. Cut apart on marked line between stitching to create two units as shown in Figure 10.

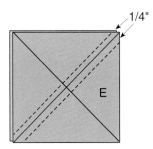

Figure 6
Stitch 1/4" on both sides of only 1 drawn line.

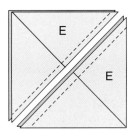

Figure 7
Cut units apart on line between stitching.

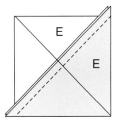

Figure 8
Extend the drawn line from the corner of 1 pink E to the corner of 1 aqua E on the wrong side of 1 unit as shown.

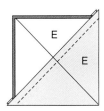

Figure 9
Match both triangle/squares with contrasting fabrics facing and marked unit on top as shown.

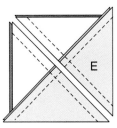

Figure 10
Cut apart on marked line between stitching to create 2 units.

13. Sew yellow print D square to an aqua end of each pieced unit. Join two units to complete one Hourglass block as shown in Figure 11; repeat for six blocks.

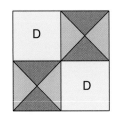

Figure 11
Join 2 units to complete 1
Hourglass block.

14. Cut 17 large pink print sashing strips 2" x 8½" for H.

15. Join two Square-in-a-Square blocks with one Hourglass block and two H strips to make a row as shown in Figure 12; repeat for two rows.

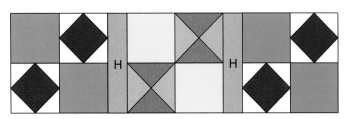

Figure 12
Join 2 Square-in-a-Square blocks with 1 Hourglass
block and 2 H strips to make a row.

16. Join two Hourglass blocks with one Square-in-a-Square block and two H strips to make a row as shown in Figure 13; repeat for two rows.

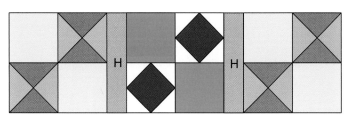

Figure 13
Join 2 Hourglass blocks with 1 Square-in-a-Square
block and 2 H strips to make a row.

17. Join three H strips with two B squares to make a sashing row as shown in Figure 14; repeat for three rows.

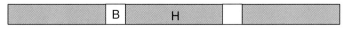

Figure 14
Join 3 H strips with 2 B squares to make a sashing row.

18. Join the block rows with the sashing rows referring to the Placement Diagram to complete pieced center; press.

19. Cut two strips each large pink print 2" x 30½" and 2" x 37". Sew the longer strips to opposite long sides and shorter strips to the top and bottom; press seams toward strips.

20. Join 26 C pieces on the 3" sides in the same color order referring to Figure 15; press seams in one direction. Repeat for two strips. Sew a strip to each long side of the pieced center; press seams toward strips.

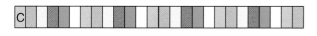

Figure 15
Join 26 C pieces on the 3" sides in the color order shown.

21. Join 20 C pieces as in step 20. Sew one F square of each color to opposite ends of each pieced strip. Sew a pieced strip to the top and bottom of the pieced center; press seams toward strips.

22. Cut and piece two strips each large pink print 6½" x 45" and 6½" x 47½". Sew the shorter strips to opposite sides and longer strips to the top and bottom of the pieced center; press seams toward strips.

23. Sandwich batting between completed top and prepared backing piece. Pin or baste layers together to hold flat.

24. Quilt as desired by hand or machine. *Note: The quilt shown was machine-quilted in the ditch of seams, through the diagonals of each block and in a meandering design on the borders using clear nylon monofilament in the top of the machine and all-purpose thread in the bobbin.* When quilting is complete, remove pins or basting; trim edges even.

25. Bind edges with self-made or purchased binding to finish. ❖

Lucy Loves Purple

BY LUCY A. FAZELY

Yes, Lucy (the designer of this quilt) certainly does love purple, and her scrap bag is full of the proof! In this quilt, she used three yards worth of purple scraps as well as a yard of a solid lavender. If purple is not your favorite color, try making this quilt in scraps of your favorite color.

Lucy Loves Purple

Project Specifications
Quilt Size: 42" x 70"
Block Size: 6" x 10"
Number of Blocks: 49

Fabric & Batting
- 1 yard lavender solid
- 3 yards total scraps purple prints
- Backing 46" x 74"
- Batting 46" x 74"
- 6½ yards self-made or purchased purple binding

Supplies & Tools
- All-purpose thread to match fabrics
- Clear nylon monofilament
- Basic sewing tools and supplies

Instructions
1. Cut 49 rectangles 6½" x 10½" from purple print

Lucy Loves Purple
6" x 10"

scraps. You will need four very dark, 16 dark, 17 medium and 12 light rectangles

2. Cut 13 strips lavender solid 2½" by fabric width. Subcut strips into 2½" segments to make squares; you will need 196 squares.

3. Draw a single diagonal line from corner to corner on the wrong side of each 2½" x 2½" lavender solid square as shown in Figure 1.

Lucy Loves Purple

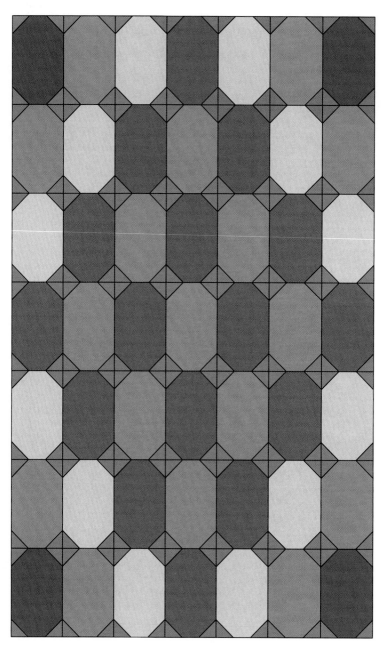

Lucy Loves Purple
Placement Diagram
42" x 70"

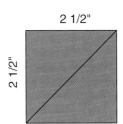

Figure 1
Draw a diagonal line
on the wrong side of
each square.

2 1/2"

2 1/2"

4. Lay a 2½" x 2½" lavender solid square on each corner of one 6½" x 10½" purple print scrap rectangle with drawn lines positioned as shown in Figure 2.

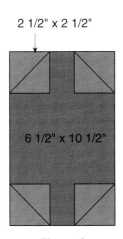

2 1/2" x 2 1/2"

6 1/2" x 10 1/2"

Figure 2
Lay squares on a
rectangle as shown.

5. Stitch along marked line on each square; trim excess to make a ¼" seam allowance as shown in Figure 3. Press seams toward triangles. Repeat for 49 blocks.

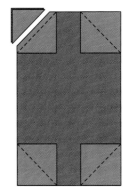

Figure 3
Trim excess to
make 1/4" seam
allowance.

6. Lay out blocks on a large clean surface to make seven rows of seven blocks each, referring to the Placement Diagram for positioning of blocks in rows.

7. Join blocks in rows; join rows to complete pieced top. Press seams in one direction.

8. Sandwich batting between completed top and prepared backing piece; pin or baste layers together.

9. Using clear nylon monofilament in the top of the machine and all-purpose thread in the bobbin, machine-quilt in the ditch of seams and meander-quilt in each rectangle.

10. When quilting is complete, trim edges even; remove pins or basting.

11. Bind edges with self-made or purchased purple binding to finish. ❖

General Instructions

Quiltmaking Basics

Materials & Supplies

Fabrics

Fabric Choices. Quilts and quilted projects combine fabrics of many types. Use same-fiber-content fabrics when making quilted items, if possible.

Buying Fabrics. One hundred percent cotton fabrics are recommended for making quilts. Choose colors similar to those used in the quilts shown or colors of your own preference. Most quilt designs depend more on contrast of values than on the colors used to create the design.

Preparing the Fabric for Use. Fabrics may be prewashed depending on your preference. Whether you prewash or not, be sure your fabrics are colorfast and won't run onto each other when washed after use.

Fabric Grain. Fabrics are woven with threads going in a crosswise and lengthwise direction. The threads cross at right angles—the more threads per inch, the stronger the fabric.

The crosswise threads will stretch a little. The lengthwise threads will not stretch at all. Cutting the fabric at a 45-degree angle to the crosswise and lengthwise threads produces a bias edge which stretches a great deal when pulled (Figure 1).

If templates are given with patterns in this book, pay careful attention to the grain lines marked with arrows. These arrows indicate that the piece should be placed on the lengthwise grain with the arrow running on one thread. Although it is not necessary to examine the fabric and find a thread to match to, it is important to try to place the arrow with the lengthwise grain of the fabric (Figure 2).

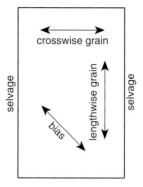

Figure 1
Drawing shows lengthwise, crosswise and bias threads.

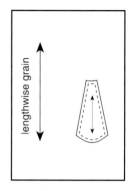

Figure 2
Place the template with marked arrow on the lengthwise grain of the fabric.

Thread

For most piecing, good-quality cotton or cotton-covered polyester is the thread of choice. Inexpensive polyester threads are not recommended because they can cut the fibers of cotton fabrics.

Choose a color thread that will match or blend with the fabrics in your quilt. For projects pieced with dark and light color fabrics choose a neutral thread color, such as a medium gray, as a compromise between colors. Test by pulling a sample seam.

Batting

Batting is the material used to give a quilt loft or thickness. It also adds warmth.

Batting size is listed in inches for each pattern to reflect the size needed to complete the quilt according to the instructions. Purchase the size large enough to cut the size you need for the quilt of your choice.

Some qualities to look for in batting are drapability, resistance to fiber migration, loft and softness.

Tools & Equipment

There are few truly essential tools and little equipment required for quiltmaking. Basics include needles (hand-sewing and quilting betweens), pins (long, thin, sharp pins are best), sharp scissors or shears, a thimble, template materials (plastic or cardboard), marking tools (chalk marker, water-erasable pen and a No. 2 pencil are a few) and a quilting frame or hoop. For piecing and/or quilting by machine, add a sewing machine to the list.

Other sewing basics such as a seam ripper, pincushion, measuring tape and an iron are also necessary. For choosing colors or quilting designs for your quilt, or for designing your own quilt, it is helpful to have on hand graph paper, tracing paper, colored pencils or markers and a ruler.

For making strip-pieced quilts, a rotary cutter, mat and specialty rulers are often used. We recommend an ergonomic rotary cutter, a large self-healing mat and several rulers. If you can choose only one size, a 6" x 24" marked in ⅛" or ¼" increments is recommended.

Construction Methods

Traditional Templates. While some quilt instructions in this book use rotary-cut strips and quick sewing methods, many patterns require a template. Templates are like the pattern pieces used to sew a garment. They are used to cut the fabric pieces that make up the quilt top. There are two types—templates that include a ¼" seam allowance and those that don't.

Choose the template material and the pattern. Transfer the pattern shapes to the template material with a sharp No. 2 lead pencil. Write the pattern name, piece letter or number, grain line and number to cut for one block or whole quilt on each piece as shown in Figure 3.

Some patterns require a reversed piece (Figure 4). These patterns are labeled with an R after the piece letter; for example, B and BR. To reverse a template, first cut it with the labeled side up and then with the labeled side down. Compare these to the right and left fronts of a blouse. When making a garment, you accomplish reversed pieces when cutting the pattern on two layers of fabric placed with right sides together. This can be done when cutting templates as well.

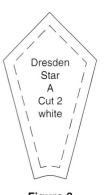

Figure 3
Mark each template with the pattern name and piece identification.

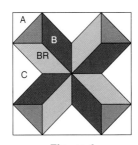

Figure 4
This pattern uses reversed pieces.

If cutting one layer of fabric at a time, first trace the template onto the backside of the fabric with the marked side down; turn the template over with the marked side up to make reverse pieces.

Hand-Piecing Basics. When hand-piecing it is easier to begin with templates that do not include the ¼" seam allowance. Place the template on the wrong side of the fabric, lining up the marked grain line with lengthwise or crosswise fabric grain. If the piece does not have to be reversed, place with labeled side up. Trace around shape; move, leaving ½" between the shapes, and mark again.

When you have marked the appropriate number of pieces, cut out pieces, leaving ¼" beyond marked line all around each piece.

To join two units, place the patches with right sides together. Stick a pin in at the beginning of the seam through both fabric patches, matching the beginning points (Figure 5); for hand-piecing, the seam begins on the traced line, not at the edge of the fabric (see Figure 6).

Figure 5
Stick a pin through fabrics to match the beginning of the seam.

Figure 6
Begin hand-piecing at seam, not at the edge of the fabric. Continue stitching along seam line.

General Instructions

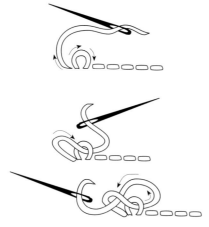

Thread a sharp needle; knot one strand of the thread at the end. Remove the pin and insert the needle in the hole; make a short stitch and then a backstitch right over the first stitch. Continue making short stitches with several stitches on the needle at one

Figure 7
Make a loop in backstitch to make a knot.

time. As you stitch, check the back piece often to assure accurate stitching on the seam line. Take a stitch at the end of the seam; backstitch and knot at the same time as shown in Figure 7. Seams on hand-pieced fabric patches may be finger-pressed toward the darker fabric.

To sew units together, pin fabric patches together, matching seams. Sew as above except where seams meet; at these intersections, backstitch, go through seam to next piece and backstitch again to secure seam joint.

Not all pieced blocks can be stitched with straight seams or in rows. Some patterns require set-in pieces. To begin a set-in seam, pin one side of the square to the proper side of the star point with right sides together, matching corners. Start stitching at the seam line on the outside point; stitch on the marked seam line to the end of the seam line at the center referring to Figure 8.

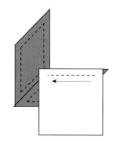

Figure 8
To set a square into a diamond point, match seams and stitch from outside edge to center.

Bring around the adjacent side and pin to the next star point, matching seams. Continue the stitching line from the adjacent seam through corners and to the outside edge of the square as shown in Figure 9.

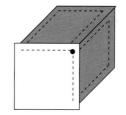

Figure 9
Continue stitching the adjacent side of the square to the next diamond shape in 1 seam from center to outside as shown.

Machine-Piecing. If making templates, include the ¼" seam allowance on the template for machine-piecing. Place template on the wrong side of the fabric as for hand-piecing except butt pieces against one another when tracing.

Set machine on 2.5 or 12–15 stitches per inch. Join pieces as for hand-piecing for set-in seams; but for other straight seams, begin and end sewing at the end of the fabric patch sewn as shown in Figure 10. No backstitching is necessary when machine-stitching.

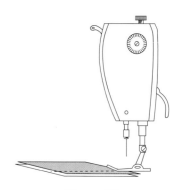

Figure 10
Begin machine-piecing at the end of the piece, not at the end of the seam.

Join units as for hand-piecing referring to the piecing diagrams where needed. Chain piecing (Figure 11—sewing several like units before sewing other units) saves time by eliminating beginning and ending stitches.

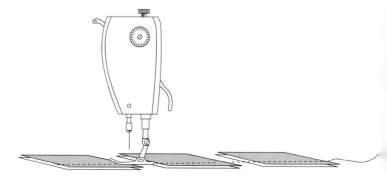

Figure 11
Units may be chain-pieced to save time.

When joining machine-pieced units, match seams against each other with seam allowances pressed in opposite directions to reduce bulk and make perfect matching of seams possible (Figure 12).

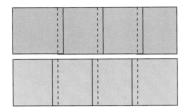

Figure 12
Sew machine-pieced units with seams
pressed in opposite directions.

Quick-Cutting. Templates can be completely eliminated when using a rotary cutter with a plastic ruler and mat to cut fabric strips.

When rotary-cutting strips, straighten raw edges of fabric by folding fabric in fourths across the width as shown in Figure 13. Press down flat; place ruler on fabric square with edge of fabric and make one cut from the folded edge to the outside edge. If strips are not straightened, a wavy strip will result as shown in Figure 14.

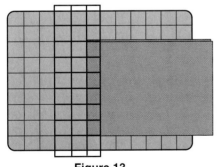

Figure 13
Fold fabric and straighten as shown.

Figure 14
Wavy strips result if fabric is not straightened before cutting.

Always cut away from your body, holding the ruler firmly with the non-cutting hand. Keep fingers away from the edge of the ruler as it is easy for the rotary cutter to slip and jump over the edge of the ruler if cutting is not properly done.

If a square is required for the pattern, it can be subcut from a strip as shown in Figure 15.

Figure 15
If cutting squares, cut proper-width strip into same-width segments. Here, a 2" strip is cut into 2" segments to create 2" squares. These squares finish at 1 1/2" when sewn.

If you need right triangles with the straight grain on the short sides, you can use the same method, but you need to figure out how wide to cut the strip. Measure the finished size of one short side of the triangle. Add ⅞" to this size for seam allowance. Cut fabric strips this width; cut the strips into the same increment to create squares. Cut the squares on the diagonal to produce triangles. For example, if you need a triangle with a 2" finished height, cut the strips 2⅞" by the width of the fabric. Cut the strips into 2⅞" squares. Cut each square on the diagonal to produce the correct-size triangle with the grain on the short sides (Figure 16).

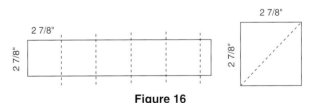

Figure 16
Cut 2" (finished size) triangles from 2 7/8" squares as shown.

Triangles sewn together to make squares are called half-square triangles or triangle/squares. When joined, the triangle/square unit has the straight of grain on all outside edges of the block.

Another method of making triangle/squares is shown in Figure 17. Layer two squares with right sides together; draw a diagonal line through the center. Stitch ¼" on both sides of the line.

General Instructions

Cut apart on the drawn line to reveal two stitched triangle/squares.

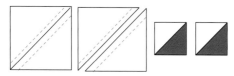

Figure 17
Mark a diagonal line on the square; stitch 1/4" on each side of the line. Cut on line to reveal stitched triangle/squares.

If you need triangles with the straight of grain on the diagonal, such as for fill-in triangles on the outside edges of a diagonal-set quilt, the procedure is a bit different.

To make these triangles, a square is cut on both diagonals; thus, the straight of grain is on the longest or diagonal side (Figure 18). To figure out the size to cut the square, add 1¼" to the needed finished size of the longest side of the triangle. For example, if you need a triangle with a 12" finished diagonal, cut a 13¼" square.

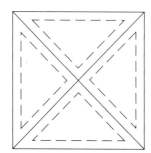

Figure 18
Add 1 1/4" to the finished size of the longest side of the triangle needed and cut on both diagonals to make a quarter-square triangle.

If templates are given, use their measurments to cut fabric strips to correspond with that measurement. The template may be used on the strip to cut pieces quickly. Strip cutting works best for squares, triangles, rectangles and diamonds. Odd-shaped templates are difficult to cut in multiple layers or using a rotary cutter.

Quick-Piecing Method. Lay pieces to be joined under the presser foot of the sewing machine right sides together. Sew an exact ¼" seam allowance to the end of the piece; place another unit right next to the first one and continue sewing, adding a piece after every stitched piece, until all of the pieces are used up (Figure 19).

Figure 19
Sew pieces together in a chain.

When sewing is finished, cut threads joining the pieces apart. Press seam toward the darker fabric.

Appliqué

Appliqué. Appliqué is the process of applying one piece of fabric on top of another for decorative or functional purposes.

Making Templates. Most appliqué designs given here are shown as full-size drawings for the completed designs. The drawings show dotted lines to indicate where one piece overlaps another. Other marks indicate placement of embroidery stitches for decorative purposes such as eyes, lips, flowers, etc.

For hand appliqué, trace each template onto the right side of the fabric with template right side up. Cut around shape, adding a ⅛"–¼" seam allowance.

Before the actual appliqué process begins, cut the background block. If you have a full-size drawing of the design, it might help you to draw on the background block to help with placement.

Transfer the design to a large piece of tracing paper. Place the paper on top of the design; use masking tape to hold in place. Trace design onto paper.

If you don't have a light box, tape the pattern on a window; center the background block on top and tape in place. Trace the design onto the background block with a water-erasable marker or light lead or chalk pencil. This drawing will mark exactly where the fabric pieces should be placed on the background block.

Hand Appliqué. Traditional hand appliqué uses a template made from the desired finished shape without seam allowance added.

After fabric is prepared, trace the desired shape onto the right side of the fabric with a water-erasable marker or light lead or chalk pencil. Leave at least ½" between design motifs when tracing to allow for the seam allowance when cutting out the shapes.

When the desired number of shapes needed has been drawn on the fabric pieces, cut out shapes leaving ⅛"–¼" all around drawn line for turning under.

Turn the shape's edges over on the drawn or stitched line. When turning in concave curves, clip to seams and baste the seam allowance over as shown in Figure 20.

Figure 20
Concave curves should be clipped before turning as shown.

During the actual appliqué process, you may be layering one shape on top of another. Where two fabrics overlap, the underneath piece does not have to be turned under or stitched down.

If possible, trim away the underneath fabric when the block is finished by carefully cutting away the background from underneath and then cutting away unnecessary layers to reduce bulk and avoid shadows from darker fabrics showing through on light fabrics.

For hand appliqué, position the fabric shapes on the background block and pin or baste them in place. Using a blind stitch or appliqué stitch, sew pieces in place with matching thread and small stitches. Start with background pieces first and work up to foreground pieces. Appliqué the pieces in place on the background in numerical order, if given, layering as necessary.

Machine Appliqué. There are several products available to help make the machine-appliqué process easier and faster.

Fusible transfer web is a commercial product similar to iron-on interfacings except it has two sticky sides. It is used to adhere appliqué shapes to the background with heat. Paper is adhered to one side of the web.

To use, reverse pattern and draw shapes onto the paper side of the web; cut, leaving a margin around each shape. Place on the wrong side of the chosen fabric; fuse in place referring to the manufacturer's instructions. Cut out shapes on the drawn line. Peel off the paper and fuse in place on the background fabric. Transfer any detail lines to the fabric shapes. This process adds a little bulk or stiffness to the appliquéd shape and makes hand-quilting through the layers difficult.

For successful machine appliqué a tear-off stabilizer is recommended. This product is placed under the background fabric while machine appliqué is being done. It is torn away when the work is finished. This kind of stabilizer keeps the background fabric from pulling during the machine-appliqué process.

During the actual machine-appliqué process, you will be layering one shape on top of another. Where two fabrics overlap, the underneath piece does not have to be turned under or stitched down.

Thread the top of the machine with thread to match the fabric patches or with threads that coordinate or contrast with fabrics. Rayon thread is a good choice when a sheen is desired on the finished appliqué stitches. Do not use rayon thread in the bobbin; use all-purpose thread.

When all machine work is complete, remove stabilizer from the back referring to the manufacturer's instructions.

Putting It All Together

Finishing the Top
Settings. Most quilts are made by sewing individual blocks together in rows that, when joined, create a design. There are several other methods used to join blocks. Sometimes the setting choice is determined by the block's design. For example, a House block should be placed upright on a quilt, not sideways or upside down.

Plain blocks can be alternated with pieced or appliquéd blocks in a straight set. Making a quilt using plain blocks saves time;

General Instructions

half the number of pieced or appliquéd blocks are needed to make the same-size quilt as shown in Figure 1.

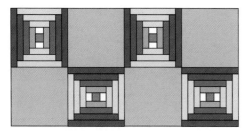

Figure 1
Alternate plain blocks with pieced blocks to save time.

Adding Borders. Borders are an integral part of the quilt and should complement the colors and designs used in the quilt center. Borders frame a quilt just like a mat and frame do a picture.

If fabric strips are added for borders, they may be mitered or butted at the corners as shown in Figures 2 and 3. To determine the size for butted border strips, measure across the center of the completed quilt top from one side raw edge to the other side raw edge. This measurement will include a ¼" seam allowance.

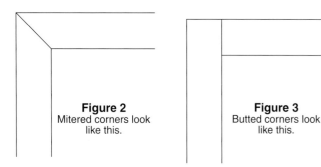

Figure 2
Mitered corners look
like this.

Figure 3
Butted corners look
like this.

Cut two border strips that length by the chosen width of the border. Sew these strips to the top and bottom of the pieced center referring to Figure 4. Press the seam allowance toward the border strips.

Measure across the completed quilt top at the center, from top raw edge to bottom raw edge, including the two border strips

already added. Cut two border strips that length by the chosen width of the border. Sew a strip to each of the two remaining sides as shown in Figure 4. Press the seams toward the border strips.

Figure 4
Sew border strips to
opposite sides; sew
remaining 2 strips to
remaining sides to make
butted corners.

To make mitered corners, measure the quilt as before. To this add twice the width of the border and ½" for seam allowances to determine the length of the strips. Repeat for opposite sides. Sew on each strip, stopping stitching ¼" from corner, leaving the remainder of the strip dangling.

Press corners at a 45-degree angle to form a crease. Stitch from the inside quilt corner to the outside on the creased line. Trim excess away after stitching and press mitered seams open (Figures 5–7).

Carefully press the entire piece, including the pieced center. Avoid pulling and stretching while pressing, which would distort shapes.

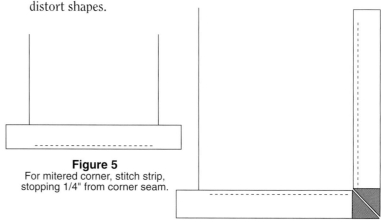

Figure 5
For mitered corner, stitch strip,
stopping 1/4" from corner seam.

Figure 6
Fold and press corner to make a
45-degree angle.

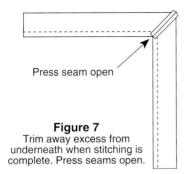

Press seam open

Figure 7
Trim away excess from
underneath when stitching is
complete. Press seams open.

Getting Ready to Quilt

Choosing a Quilting Design. If you choose to hand- or machine-quilt your finished top, you will need to select a design for quilting.

There are several types of quilting designs, some of which may not have to be marked. The easiest of the unmarked designs is in-the-ditch quilting. Here the quilting stitches are placed in the valley created by the seams joining two pieces together or next to the edge of an appliqué design. There is no need to mark a top for in-the-ditch quilting. Machine quilters choose this option because the stitches are not as obvious on the finished quilt. (Figure 8).

Outline-quilting ¼" or more away from seams or appliqué shapes is another no-mark alternative (Figure 9) that prevents having to sew through the layers made by seams, thus making stitching easier.

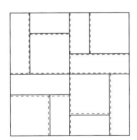

Figure 8
In-the-ditch quilting is done in
the seam that joins 2 pieces.

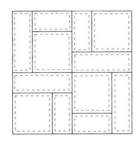

Figure 9
Outline-quilting 1/4" away
from seam is a popular
choice for quilting.

If you are not comfortable eyeballing the ¼" (or other distance), masking tape is available in different widths and is helpful to place on straight-edge designs to mark the quilting line. If using masking tape, place the tape right up against the seam and quilt close to the other edge.

Meander or free-motion quilting by machine fills in open spaces and doesn't require marking. It is fun and easy to stitch as shown in Figure 10.

Marking the Top for Quilting. If you choose a fancy or allover design for quilting, you will need to transfer the design to your quilt top before layering with the backing and batting. You may use a sharp medium-lead or silver pencil on light background fabrics. Test the pencil marks to guarantee that they will wash out of your quilt top when quilting is complete; or be sure your quilting stitches cover the pencil marks. Mechanical pencils with very fine points may be used successfully to mark quilts.

Figure 10
Machine meander quilting
fills in large spaces.

Manufactured quilt-design templates are available in many designs and sizes and are cut out of a durable plastic template material that is easy to use.

To make a permanent quilt-design template, choose a template material on which to transfer the design. See-through plastic is the best as it will let you place the design while allowing you to see where it is in relation to your quilt design without moving it. Place the design on the quilt top where you want it and trace around it with your marking tool. Pick up the quilting template and place again; repeat marking.

No matter what marking method you use, remember—the marked lines should never show on the finished quilt. When the top is marked, it is ready for layering.

Preparing the Quilt Backing. The quilt backing is a very important feature of your quilt. The materials listed for each quilt in this book includes the size requirements for the backing, not the yardage needed. Exceptions to this are when the backing fabric is also used on the quilt top and yardage is given for that fabric.

A backing is generally cut at least 4" larger than the quilt top or 2" larger on all sides. For a 64" x 78" finished quilt, the backing would need to be at least 68" x 82".

To avoid having the seam across the center of the quilt

General Instructions

backing, cut or tear one of the right-length pieces in half and sew half to each side of the second piece as shown in Figure 11.

Quilts that need a backing more than 88" wide may be pieced in horizontal pieces as shown in Figure 12.

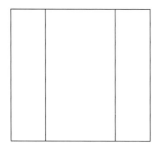

Figure 11
Center 1 backing piece with a piece on each side.

Figure 12
Horizontal seams may be used on backing pieces.

Layering the Quilt Sandwich. Layering the quilt top with the batting and backing is time-consuming. Open the batting several days before you need it and place over a bed or flat on the floor to help flatten the creases caused from its being folded up in the bag for so long.

Iron the backing piece, folding in half both vertically and horizontally and pressing to mark centers.

If you will not be quilting on a frame, place the backing right side down on a clean floor or table. Start in the center and push any wrinkles or bunches flat. Use masking tape to tape the edges to the floor or large clips to hold the backing to the edges of the table. The backing should be taut.

Place the batting on top of the backing, matching centers using fold lines as guides; flatten out any wrinkles. Trim the batting to the same size as the backing.

Fold the quilt top in half lengthwise and place on top of the batting, wrong side against the batting, matching centers. Unfold quilt and, working from the center to the outside edges, smooth out any wrinkles or lumps.

To hold the quilt layers together for quilting, baste by hand or use safety pins. If basting by hand, thread a long thin needle with a long piece of unknotted white or off-white thread. Starting in the center and leaving a long tail, make 4"–6" stitches toward the outside edge of the quilt top, smoothing as you baste. Start at the center again and work toward the outside as shown in Figure 13.

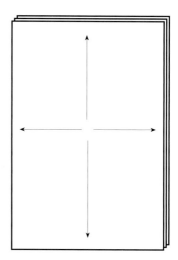

Figure 13
Baste from the center to the outside edges.

If quilting by machine, you may prefer to use safety pins for holding your fabric sandwich together. Start in the center of the quilt and pin to the outside, leaving pins open until all are placed. When you are satisfied that all layers are smooth, close the pins.

Quilting
Hand Quilting. Hand quilting is the process of placing stitches through the quilt top, batting and backing to hold them

together. While it is a functional process, it also adds beauty and loft to the finished quilt.

To begin, thread a sharp between needle with an 18" piece of quilting thread. Tie a small knot in the end of the thread. Position the needle about ½" to 1" away from the starting point on quilt top. Sink the needle through the top into the batting layer but not through the backing. Pull the needle up at the starting point of the quilting design. Pull the needle and thread until the knot sinks through the top into the batting (Figure 14).

Some stitchers like to take a backstitch here at the beginning while others prefer to begin the first stitch here. Take small, even running stitches along the marked quilting line (Figure 15). Keep one hand positioned underneath to feel the needle go all the way through to the backing.

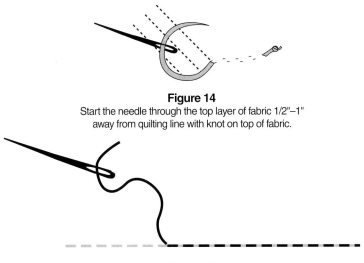

Figure 14
Start the needle through the top layer of fabric 1/2"–1" away from quilting line with knot on top of fabric.

Figure 15
Make small, even running stitches on marked quilting line.

When you have nearly run out of thread, wind the thread around the needle several times to make a small knot and pull it close to the fabric. Insert the needle into the fabric on the quilting line and come out with the needle ½" to 1" away, pulling the knot into the fabric layers the same as when you started. Pull and cut thread close to fabric. The end should disappear inside after cutting. Some quilters prefer to take a backstitch with a loop through it for a knot to end.

Machine Quilting. Successful machine quilting requires practice and a good relationship with your sewing machine.

Prepare the quilt for machine quilting in the same way as for hand quilting. Use safety pins to hold the layers together instead of basting with thread.

Presser-foot quilting is best used for straight-line quilting because the presser bar lever does not need to be continually lifted.

Set the machine on a longer stitch length (3.0 or 8–10 stitches to the inch). Too tight a stitch causes puckering and fabric tucks, either on the quilt top or backing. An even-feed or walking foot helps to eliminate the tucks and puckering by feeding the upper and lower layers through the machine evenly. Before you begin, loosen the amount of pressure on the presser foot.

Special machine-quilting needles work best to penetrate the three layers in your quilt.

Decide on a design. Quilting in the ditch is not quite as visible, but if you quilt with the feed dogs engaged, it means turning the quilt frequently. It is not easy to fit a rolled-up quilt through the small opening on the sewing machine head.

Meander quilting is the easiest way to machine-quilt—and it is fun. Meander quilting is done using an appliqué or darning foot with the feed dogs dropped. It is sort of like scribbling. Simply move the quilt top around under the foot and make stitches in a random pattern to fill the space. The same method may be used to outline a quilt design. The trick is the same as in hand quilting; you are striving for stitches of uniform size. Your hands are in complete control of the design.

If machine quilting is of interest to you, there are several very good books available at quilt shops that will help you become a successful machine quilter.

Finishing the Edges

After your quilt is tied or quilted, the edges need to be finished. Decide how you want the edges of your quilt finished before layering the backing and batting with the quilt top.

Without Binding—Self-Finish. There is one way to eliminate adding an edge finish. This is done before quilting. Place the batting on a flat surface. Place the pieced top right side up on the batting. Place the backing right sides together with the pieced top. Pin and/or baste the layers together to hold flat referring to Layering the Quilt Sandwich.

General Instructions

Begin stitching in the center of one side using a ¼" seam allowance, reversing at the beginning and end of the seam. Continue stitching all around and back to the beginning side. Leave a 12" or larger opening. Clip corners to reduce excess. Turn right side out through the opening. Slipstitch the opening closed by hand. The quilt may now be quilted by hand or machine.

The disadvantage to this method is that once the edges are sewn in, any creases or wrinkles that might form during the quilting process cannot be flattened out. Tying is the preferred method for finishing a quilt constructed using this method.

Bringing the backing fabric to the front is another way to finish the quilt's edge without binding. To accomplish this, complete the quilt as for hand or machine quilting. Trim the batting only even with the front. Trim the backing 1" larger than the completed top all around.

Turn the backing edge in ½" and then turn over to the front along edge of batting. The folded edge may be machine-stitched close to the edge through all layers, or blind-stitched in place to finish.

The front may be turned to the back. If using this method, a wider front border is needed. The backing and batting are trimmed 1" smaller than the top and the top edge is turned under ½" and then turned to the back and stitched in place.

One more method of self-finish may be used. The top and backing may be stitched together by hand at the edge. To accomplish this, all quilting must be stopped ½" from the quilt-top edge. The top and backing of the quilt are trimmed even and the batting is trimmed to ¼"–½" smaller. The edges of the top and backing are turned in ¼"–½" and blind-stitched together at the very edge.

These methods do not require the use of extra fabric and save time in preparation of binding strips; they are not as durable as an added binding.

Binding. The technique of adding extra fabric at the edges of the quilt is called binding. The binding encloses the edges and adds an extra layer of fabric for durability.

To prepare the quilt for the addition of the binding, trim the batting and backing layers flush with the top of the quilt using a rotary cutter and ruler or shears. Using a walking-foot attachment (sometimes called an even-feed foot attachment), machine-baste the three layers together all around approximately ⅛" from the cut edge.

The materials listed for each quilt in this book often includes a number of yards of self-made or purchased binding. Bias binding may be purchased in packages and in many colors. The advantage to self-made binding is that you can use fabrics from your quilt to coordinate colors. Double-fold, straight-grain binding and double-fold, bias-grain binding are two of the most commonly used types of binding.

Double-fold, straight-grain binding is used on smaller projects with right-angle corners. Double-fold, bias-grain binding is best suited for bed-size quilts or quilts with rounded corners.

To make double-fold, straight-grain binding, cut 2¼"-wide strips of fabric across the width or down the length of the fabric totaling the perimeter of the quilt plus 10". The strips are joined as shown in Figure 16 and pressed in half wrong sides together along the length using an iron on a cotton setting with no steam.

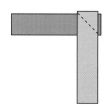

Figure 16
Join binding strips in a
diagonal seam to eliminate
bulk as shown.

Lining up the raw edges, place the binding on the top of the quilt and begin sewing (again using the walking foot) approximately 6" from the beginning of the binding strip. Stop sewing ¼" from the first corner, leave the needle in the quilt, turn and sew diagonally to the corner as shown in Figure 17.

Fold the binding at a 45-degree angle up and away from the quilt as shown in Figure 18 and back down flush with the raw edges. Starting at the top raw edge of the quilt, begin sewing the next side as shown in Figure 19. Repeat at the next three corners.

As you approach the beginning of the binding strip, stop stitching and overlap the binding ½" from the edge; trim. Join the two ends with a ¼" seam allowance and press the seam open. Reposition the joined binding along the edge of the quilt and resume stitching to the beginning.

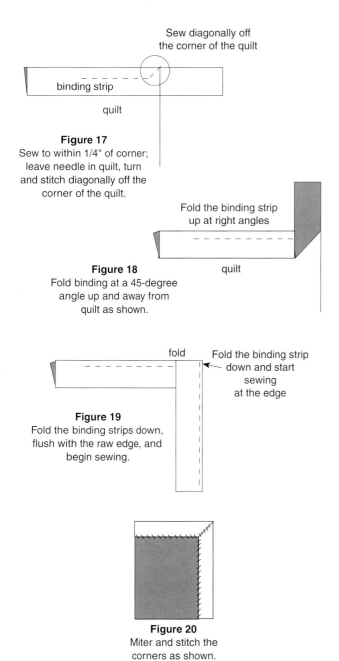

Sew diagonally off
the corner of the quilt

binding strip

quilt

Figure 17
Sew to within 1/4" of corner;
leave needle in quilt, turn
and stitch diagonally off the
corner of the quilt.

Fold the binding strip
up at right angles

quilt

Figure 18
Fold binding at a 45-degree
angle up and away from
quilt as shown.

fold

Fold the binding strip
down and start
sewing
at the edge

Figure 19
Fold the binding strips down,
flush with the raw edge, and
begin sewing.

Figure 20
Miter and stitch the
corners as shown.

To finish, bring the folded edge of the binding over the raw edges and blind-stitch the binding in place over the machine-stitching line on the backside. Hand-miter the corners on the back as shown in Figure 20.

If you are making a quilt to be used on a bed, you may want to use double-fold, bias-grain bindings because the many threads that cross each other along the fold at the edge of the quilt make it a more durable binding.

Cut 2¼"-wide bias strips from a large square of fabric. Join the strips as illustrated in Figure 16 and press the seams open. Fold the beginning end of the bias strip ¼" from the raw edge and press. Fold the joined strips in half along the long side, wrong sides together, and press with no steam (Figure 21).

Figure 21
Fold and press strip in half.

Follow the same procedures as previously described for preparing the quilt top and sewing the binding to the quilt top. Treat the corners just as you treated them with straight-grain binding.

Since you are using bias-grain binding, you do have the option to just eliminate the corners if this option doesn't interfere with the patchwork in the quilt. Round the corners off by placing one of your dinner plates at the corner and rotary-cutting the gentle curve (Figure 22).

Figure 22
Round corners to eliminate
square-corner finishes.

As you approach the beginning of the binding strip, stop stitching and lay the end across the beginning so it will slip inside the fold. Cut the end at a 45-degree angle so the raw edges are contained inside the beginning of the strip (Figure 23). Resume stitching to the beginning. Bring the fold to the back of the quilt and hand-stitch as previously described.

Figure 23
End the binding strips as shown.

Overlapped corners are not quite as easy as rounded ones, but a bit easier than mitering. To make overlapped corners, sew binding strips to opposite sides of the quilt top. Stitch edges down to finish. Trim ends even.

Sew a strip to each remaining side, leaving 1½"–2" excess at each end. Turn quilt over and fold binding down even with previous finished edge as shown in Figure 24.

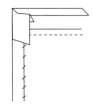

Figure 24
Fold end of binding even with
previous page.

Fold binding in toward quilt and stitch down as before, enclosing the previous bound edge in the seam as shown in Figure 25. It may be necessary to trim the folded-down section to reduce bulk.

Figure 25
An overlapped corner is not quite as
neat as a mitered corner.

Final Touches

If your quilt will be hung on the wall, a hanging sleeve is required. Other options include purchased plastic rings or fabric tabs. The best choice is a fabric sleeve, which will evenly distribute the weight of the quilt across the top edge, rather than at selected spots where tabs or rings are stitched, keep the quilt hanging straight and not damage the batting.

To make a sleeve, measure across the top of the finished quilt. Cut an 8"-wide piece of muslin equal to that length—you may need to seam several muslin strips together to make the required length.

Fold in ¼" on each end of the muslin strip and press. Fold again and stitch to hold. Fold the muslin strip lengthwise with right sides together. Sew along the long side to make a tube. Turn the tube right side out; press with seam at bottom or centered on the back.

Hand-stitch the tube along the top of the quilt and the bottom of the tube to the quilt back making sure the quilt lies flat. Stitches should not go through to the front of the quilt and don't need to be too close together as shown in Figure 26.

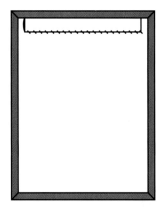

Figure 26
Sew a sleeve to the top back of the quilt.

Slip a wooden dowel or long curtain rod through the sleeve to hang.

When the quilt is finally complete, it should be signed and dated. Use a permanent pen on the back of the quilt. Other methods include cross-stitching your name and date on the front or back or making a permanent label which may be stitched to the back.